WordPress for Beginners 2020

A Visual Step-by-Step Guide to Mastering WordPress

Updated 18th December 2019

What people are saying about previous versions of this book:

"I work in the education department at one of the top academic institutions in the U.S. and if I could hire Dr. Williams to write all of my online training, I wouldn't hesitate..." **Laurie**

"Wow! From someone who is not a beginner to WordPress." **Albert J**

"Definitely the go-to guide! Since WordPress is a pretty easy format to get started on, I was able to make some progress. Then I found WordPress for Beginners and WOW - my progress took off. Having a visual guide with extensive photos really helps those of us who are visual learners. But the best thing to me is that Williams not only describes what to do and how to do it, he explains why you should do it. I'm not a professional tech person and this book is exactly what I needed. I suspect I will continue to refer to it in the future. Highly recommended." **Amazon Customer**

"Nailed It. I have been trying to install a working blog from time to time for the last four years, and of course, have read various books on the subject. It always got more complicated, with dashboards, PHP, SQL, SEO, or a shared WordPress site. This is the one book that does it flawlessly, and the installation actually works just as shown. The screenshots are accurate and most helpful as you step through each learning segment. Having written several technical how-to manuals myself, I recognize a remarkably well structured and logical sequence of easy to learn, bite-sized topics." **Terry O'Hara**

"If you want to have a website but don't know how, this book by Dr. Andy Williams will take you by the hand and walk you through the process of setting up your own blog correctly. He tells you not only exactly how to do it, but also explains the why you are taking the steps he walks you through. The instructions and visuals are clear and easy for anyone to follow." **J. Tanner**

"I Would Give This Book a 5 Plus. I literally started at page one and built my website from scratch without any prior experience because of this book. It was very easy to read and was laid out in a very logical, step by step order. I would recommend it without hesitation. I was so impressed with this book that I went and ordered several other of the author's books relating to developing an online presence." **GP**

"Clear, practical, and very helpful, WordPress for Beginners takes the reader step by step through the essentials of organizing your online world. Dr. Williams is a great writer and an excellent teacher. Highly recommended!" **Dr. James A. Holmund**

"Great lessons from a great teacher. Andy Williams really has a knack for organizing information in a clear, concise, and to-the-point manner. It is only a matter of following his excellent advice, and you will have a functioning WordPress site up and running in no time." **Prufrock**

"Why can't all guides be like this?" **B J Burton**

"Exemplary teaching. This book is a model of good teaching. Clear, uncluttered, direct. It takes you through the process with admirable clarity. I bought a printed guide to Word Press for twice the price which left me utterly confused - this book should be used as an example of how to teach. Very highly recommended." **Amazon Customer**

"An excellent book. I logged into my account and just followed the book page by page and in no time at all I had a Website mapped out and running. The book is easy to follow and you very quickly learn how WordPress works and how it can be used for writing Blogs, conventional Websites and even combined ones if you are so inclined. This really is an excellent book to have in your programming library and is of great value in helping to steer through the morass of misinformation about WordPress on the web. I have just ordered the paperback version to have by my side which I anticipate will become well-worn into the future." **Dr. A F Gerrard**

"Quite simply the best advice I've found............ Having spent a number of months getting disheartened and frustrated, I bought this book as a last-ditch attempt to get my website going before having to pay someone to do it for me. Setting up a website is not something I'd ever done before so I had no technical knowledge at all. Quite simply, this book is superb. It was just like having the web developer sitting next to me at my desk talking me through every little detail. He 'told me' what to ignore (explaining why as he did so), explained what we were doing and why at every step and the pictures aligned to what was on my screen as I went along. Two days later I had a website and now I am actually changing the theme and altering things with confidence. I simply cannot rate this book highly enough. Thank you, Andy!" **Louise Burridge**

"Brilliant - all you need to know to get up and running." **S. J. Oswald**

"I had to design a website urgently and one I could manage myself. I'd read that to do this I needed a web design programme that offered CMS, Content Control Management and that WordPress was the best programme for the job. I was a complete beginner with no knowledge at all about website design. Before I came across Dr. Andy Williams's book I'd bought two others and became overwhelmed by the complexity and the jargon.

If you want to design your own website, you don't need any other book than this. If you work through it carefully and methodically you'll quickly learn all the technicalities involved and have the vocabulary to create a website that is visually arresting, the content, of course, is up to you.

Dr. Williams is a natural-born teacher with that special genius of being able to make a complex process easy and interesting to follow. The large-format book is a pleasure to use. It begins with the assumption that the reader knows nothing about WordPress, website hosting, registering and costs. The easy to follow steps takes you through this process to the point where once your website is up and running, the reader can download WordPress, then get to work! Dr. Williams takes you through every aspect of the WordPress 'dashboard,' (the programme's control panel) a place it is important to know well, and where the web designer will spend a lot of time. Once the reader is familiar with this, the design process starts and Dr. Williams again leads the reader step by step through the website building process.

One of the many outstanding features of the book is the use of screenshots that show the reader what to do and where to do it, it's like using a print out of a video. Another indispensable feature is the "Tasks to Complete" sections found at the end of each major learning phase. The reader is given a list of tasks to work through which consolidates what has been learned and offers a comprehensive revision structure that can be revisited as many times as necessary.

"WordPress for Beginners" is not just an outstanding book about WordPress, it is also a model of how this kind of "teaching at a distance," should be done. Dr. Williams has written several other books using the same teaching techniques, we can only hope the list continues to grow."
Dr. Gerald Benedict

Disclaimer and Terms of Use Agreement

The author and publisher of this eBook and the accompanying materials have used their best efforts in preparing this eBook. The author and publisher make no representation or warranties with respect to the accuracy, applicability, fitness, or completeness of the contents of this eBook. The information contained in this eBook is strictly for educational purposes. Therefore, if you wish to apply ideas contained in this eBook, you are taking full responsibility for your actions.

The author and publisher disclaim any warranties (express or implied), merchantability, or fitness for any particular purpose. The author and publisher shall in no event be held liable to any party for any direct, indirect, punitive, special, incidental or other consequential damages arising directly or indirectly from any use of this material, which is provided "as is", and without warranties.

The author and publisher do not warrant the performance, effectiveness or applicability of any sites listed or linked to in this eBook.

All links are for information purposes only and are not warranted for content, accuracy or any other implied or explicit purpose.

The author and publisher of this book are not in any way associated with Google.

Contents

A Little Bit of History

In the early days, websites were hand-built using a code called Hypertext Markup Language, or HTML for short. To create good-looking websites, you needed to be something of a geek. Tools like Macromedia Dreamweaver (now owned by Adobe) and Microsoft Front Page (discontinued in 2006) were developed to reduce the learning curve associated with building a website in HTML, but these tools were expensive.

Then in May 2003, Matt Mullenweg & Mike Little released a tool that would change the face of website building forever. They called it WordPress. I have to admit I was a little reluctant to give up my copy of Dreamweaver, but in 2004 I started to experiment with the WordPress platform. At that time, WordPress was just starting to get interesting with the introduction of "plugins". Don't worry, we'll look at those later in the book, but for now, just understand that plugins are an easy and pain-free way of adding great new functionality to your website.

Fast-forward to today and WordPress is now the site-building tool of choice for many professionals and enthusiasts alike. Home businesses run by moms & dads, school kids running blogs about their favorite bands, large corporations, and everyone in between, have all turned to WordPress. It's extremely powerful, flexible, produces very professional looking websites or blogs, is relatively easy to use, and perhaps best of all, it's totally free. Sure, there is a learning curve, but that is where I come in.

With years of experience teaching technical stuff in an easy to understand manner, I am going to take you by the hand and guide you as you construct your very own professional looking website or blog, even if you know absolutely nothing about how to go about this. The only thing you need to know is how to use a web browser. If you have ever searched Google for something, then you already have the skills necessary to follow this book.

I have made this book a step-by-step, visual guide to creating your website. Just follow along with the exercises and in no time at all, you'll be using WordPress like a pro. You'll build a website you can be proud to show your family and friends. In fact, they will probably start asking YOU to help them build their own website.

Excited? OK, let's get on with it.

How to Use This Book

I do not recommend you just sit down and read this book. The problem is that a lot of this book describes processes that you actually need to do on your computer. If you try to read, without following along on your computer, you will get lost and not be too sure what I am talking about.

This book is a hands-on tutorial. To get the most out of it, I recommend that you sit at your computer with the book open in front of you, and follow along as you work your way through.

I'll use screenshots in the book that best demonstrate the point. These may be from a couple of my own real sites, or a demo site I have installed on my own computer.

Whenever I do something on my demo site, you should try it on your own site. Don't be afraid of making mistakes; just have fun and experiment with WordPress. Mistakes can easily be undone or deleted, and anyway, most of us learn better by making a few blunders along the way.

By the end of this book, you will have a solid understanding of how WordPress works and how you can get it to do what YOU want it to do. If you then decide to take your WordPress knowledge to the next level, you'll have an excellent foundation from which to build upon.

Towards the end of the book is a section called "Types of WordPress Websites. This section will highlight the flexibility of WordPress as a site creation tool, by showing you how to use WordPress to build a typical website, a business site, and a blog. I'll provide you with links to videos showing how to structure each of these types of site using WordPress. Use these videos together with the content of this book to design the type of site you want.

Updates & Changes to WordPress?

When this book was written, the current version of WordPress was 5.3. However, the WordPress ecosystem changes a lot, and while most of these changes will be minor (you may not even notice them), some bigger changes can happen. After this book is published, there isn't much I can do to notify you of these changes. I have therefore set up a page on my website for book owners, so that updates, changes, and issues, can be listed. If something in the book does not look right, visit the updates page here:

https://ezseonews.com/wp2020/

You can leave comments on that page if you need to.

Yes, that is the exact same free WordPress.com website after applying the hack.

The dashboard now looks almost identical to the one that WordPress.org users (and this book) see, and that means you can follow most of this book as you explore and learn to use WordPress.

To apply the hack, login to your WordPress.com dashboard. Have a look at the address bar of your browser. It will look something like this:

Delete "wordpress.com/home/" from the start of that URL and press the return key on your keyboard. That will take you to your homepage.

Now add the following to the end of the URL:

/wp-admin

.. and press the return key on your keyword.

It should look like this:

You should see the new look dashboard shown earlier.

You now have a Dashboard that is very similar to the one in the WordPress.org version of WordPress. You can now follow most of the instructions in this book.

Be aware that the limitations are still present. You will be restricted in what you can do on the site, and what you can install into WordPress. That is the price you pay for using the free version. Not everything I describe in this book will be available to you.

My recommendation is to use the WordPress.org version. If you have a WordPress.com website that you want to convert to a hosted WordPress.org site, I've included a chapter at the end of this book explaining the process of moving the site.

WordPress.org

WordPress.org is a site where you can download your own copy of WordPress for free. You can then upload that copy of WordPress to any web server you like and start building a site that YOU own. You will also be able to choose whatever domain name you like, so you could call your site educationaltoysforkids.com (if it's available). Doesn't that look more professional than the options on WordPress.com?

Think of the difference between WordPress.com and WordPress.org as being similar to renting or owning a house. When you rent a house, there are limits to what you can do to it. You can be thrown out at any time. When you own the building outright, you can do whatever you want with it and no one can tell you how to design, decorate, or renovate *your* home.

The only disadvantages of using WordPress.org are the costs involved. These costs are minimal though, so let's look at them.

The Costs of Owning Your Own Site

So how much is a website going to cost you? As you build your site there will be optional costs - things like a website theme, autoresponder or mailing list, but these are totally optional since most things can be done for free. However, there are two costs that you cannot avoid.

The Website Domain

The website domain is your site's address on the internet. **Google.com** is the website domain of our favorite search engine. **CNN.com** is the domain of a popular international news service.

You will need to buy a domain for your website. We'll look at this later, but for now, let's just consider the price. Typically, a domain name will cost around $10 per year. You can sometimes get the first year for free when you buy web hosting, but once that first year is up, you'll be paying the $10 per year to keep your domain name alive.

Your domain name will be registered with a company called a registrar. It is the registrar that will collect the $10 payment every year. The registrar can be the same company that you use for your web hosting or a different company. We'll look at the pros and cons of both options later.

Website Hosting

Your website needs to be "hosted" on a special type of computer called a server. Servers are connected to the internet 24/7. We call the companies that lease or rent space out on these servers "web hosts". A web host's job is to make sure their servers are up, running, and well maintained, at all times.

Since you want to create a website, you need to rent some disk space from a web host, on one of these servers. This is a monthly fee starting around $3.99 - $5.00 per month (although it does vary greatly between web hosts).

As mentioned earlier, some web hosts offer a free domain name (for the first year). They can offer a free domain name because you are paying them a monthly fee for web hosting; therefore, they get their investment back over time. To take advantage of the free domain offers, you will need to use that web host as the registrar of your domain, which I don't recommend (see later).

So, the total essential costs of running your own website are:

1. $10 per year for the domain name.
2. $5 per month for web hosting.

That´s a total of around $70 per year.

Registrar & Web Hosts

When you sign up with a web host, they will offer to be your domain registrar as well. The advantage is that all the bills you receive are from the same company, meaning you only have to deal with ONE company.

There are disadvantages to this arrangement though, and a lot of people (including myself), prefer to keep host and registrar separate.

Potential problem: If for any reason your web host decides your website is causing them problems (i.e. they get spam complaints, or your website is using up too many system resources), they can take your site down without any warning. What happens next?

If you use a combined web host and registrar, it goes something like this:

1. Your site goes down.
2. You contact your host and they tell you that they received spam complaints about your domain.
3. They refuse to put your site back up.
4. You need to move your site to a new host, but your existing web host is the registrar and can make that difficult.
5. Your site remains down for a long period of time while you sort things out, and eventually move the site to a new host and registrar.

Time to resolve this? Weeks or months.

OK, let's see what happens if your registrar is separate from your host.

1. Your site goes down.
2. You contact your host and they tell you that they received spam complaints from your domain.
3. They refuse to put your site back up.
4. You order hosting with a different company, and copy your site to the new host.
5. You log in to your registrar account and change the name servers (don't worry about this, we'll look at it later), to the new host. This takes seconds to do.

Time to resolve this? Your site is back up within 24 hours or less, on the new web host.

This is one scenario where using a separate host and registrar is important.

Another scenario, which doesn't bear thinking about, is if your hosting company goes out of business (it does happen sometimes). What becomes of your site? Well, you probably lose it AND your domain name if your hosting company is also your registrar.

If your registrar and host are two separate companies, you'd simply get hosting somewhere else and change the name servers at your registrar. With this arrangement, your site would only be down for 24 hours or less.

Another situation that I have heard about is when a hosting company locks you out of your control panel (a login area where you can administer your domain(s)), because of a dispute over something.

That means you cannot possibly move the domain to a new host because you must have access to that control panel to do it. Consequently, your domain will be down for as long as the dispute takes to resolve.

A final word of caution! I have heard horror stories of people not being able to transfer their domain out from a bad web host. Even worse than that, the domain they registered at the hosting company was not registered in their name, but in the name of the hosting company.

For all of the above reasons, when you are ready to buy hosting, please consider the separate web host and registrar that I personally use and recommend.

If you just want the easy option of using one company, use the web host I recommend. I have used them for years (sometimes as a combined host and registrar on a few sites) and never had a problem.

Recommended Registrars & Web Hosts

Since the prices, features, etc. of web hosts can change so quickly, I have created a page on my website that lists my recommended web host and registrar.

The page also has a link to a comparative review where I show the reliability and speed of my recommended host, compared to another popular web host.

https://ezseonews.com/dwh

Tasks to Complete

Read the web page above. This will give you instructions on which registrar and host to use, and how to set everything up.

1. Sign up at the recommended registrar (it's free) and buy your domain name.
2. Sign up for the recommended web hosting by following the instructions on that web page. A web host will try to get you to buy the domain from them, but you already have yours, so that web page shows how to set this all up. After following the instructions on that page, you will have bought your domain at the registrar, bought separate web hosting, and connected the two. The next step is installing WordPress.

Installing WordPress

For this, you need to login to the cPanel of your hosting. The URL, username, and password were all in the welcome email the host sent you when you signed up.

Installing the SSL certificate

To make your site secure and trusted by your visitors, you want web browsers to show a padlock symbol in the address bar.

To have this padlock, you need to install an SSL certificate on your server. If you are using a host that supports Let's Encrypt (like the host I use and recommend in this book), then this is easy. If your host does not support Let's Encrypt (or you are buying an SSL certificate), then you'll need to ask them about installing an SSL certificate (though they may charge for it).

I am going to assume your host supports Let's Encrypt.

Login to cPanel.

Scroll down to the **Security** section, and click on the **Let's Encrypt** SSL link.

You'll see a list of all Let's Encrypt SSL certificates that have been installed on your account in the "Your domains with Let's Encrypt™ certificates". You'll also see a section called "Issue a new certificate".

If you don't see your domain in the list of domains with Let's Encrypt certificates, then you'll need to issue one.

Scroll down to the "Issue a new certificate" section, and find your domain in the list.

Issue a new certificate

Choose from one of your domains below. A new key and certificate will be added to the SSL/TLS manager.

Show 10 ▼ entries

Domain		Alt Names		Actions

andyjwilliams.co.uk, andyjwilliams.harlun.co.uk,

harlunlimited.com   harlunlimited.com, harlunlimited.harlun.co.uk, mail.harlunlimited.com, www.harlunlimited.com, www.harlunlimited.harlun.co.uk,   ➕ Issue

To the right, click the link to "Issue".

You'll get a page with some options, but leave everything set at the default values and click the **Issue** button.

OK, that's done. cPanel has created and installed the SSL certificate on your server. You are now ready to install WordPress on your server. Head back to cPanel by clicking the dial button top left:

Installing WordPress

Scroll down to the **Software** section, and click on the **Softaculous app installer.** Please note that depending on the version (and skin) of cPanel you are using, your screen may look a little different to mine.

Your cPanel may even have a dedicated section called **Softaculous Apps Installer**, which looks like this:

This panel, if you have it, allows you to jump straight to the WordPress install screen by clicking on the WordPress button.

If you clicked the link in the **Software** section, you'll have an extra button to click. Look for the WordPress button:

Move your mouse over it, and an **Install** button will appear:

WordPress is a state-of-the-art publishing platform with a focus on aesthetics, web standards, and usability.

Install   Demo   Overview

WordPress
★★★★☆

Click the **Install** button.

At the top of the next screen, you'll see this:

Software Setup   Quick Install

Choose the version you want to install   5.2.4   ▾
Please select the version to install.

Choose Installation URL   https:// ▾   harlunlimited.com   ▾
Please choose the URL to install the software
                                           Choose Protocol   Choose Domain ⓘ   In Directory ⓘ

In the **Choose Protocol** box, make sure **https://** is selected.

In the **"Choose Domain"** box, select the domain where you want to install WordPress.

NOTE: If you see this message after selecting a domain:

ⓘ
A trusted SSL Certificate was not found

.. it means that no SSL certificate was found.

If you followed the steps earlier to install a Let's Encrypt certificate, give it 10 minutes and come back and try again. On the other hand, if you could not install an SSL certificate at this time, but want to continue installing Wordpress, choose HTTP as the protocol instead of HTTPS and continue with the installation.

The **"In Directory"** box should be empty.

Next, we have these settings:

Site Settings

Site Name   My Blog

Site Description   My WordPress Blog

Enable Multisite (WPMU) ⓘ   ☐   ⬅

Enter a name & description for your site. You can change these later, so don't worry too much about it.

Leave Enable Multisite (WPMU) unchecked.

Next, we have the Admin account settings:

Admin Account

Admin Username		⚙
Admin Password		⚙ Hide
	Strong (65/100)	🔑
Admin Email	admin@harlunlimited.com	⚙

The fields in this section come pre-populated with a secure username and password. You can change these if you want, but:

1. Don't use admin as your username.
2. Use a strong password.

You can check how strong your password is with the visual indicator underneath the password box. Use upper and lower characters, numbers, and special characters. If you are worried about remembering the password, do a Google search for password managers, and use one. They'll remember and fill passwords for you. I personally use one called Sticky Password, but LastPass or Roboform are other good options. The username and password combination entered here will be used to login to your WordPress Dashboard, so make a note of them. Do not proceed until you have made a copy of these details.

The "Admin email" box will set the admin email in your WordPress dashboard. This will be used to notify you of events, like people leaving comments. This can be changed later but make sure it is a valid email address before you continue. If you did forget your password, this is the email address that will be used to reset the password.

By default, the language will be set to English, but change this if you need to.

Choose Language

| Select Language | English ▼ |

Softaculous can install a useful plugin for you:

Select Plugin(s)

Manage Plugin Sets

Limit Login Attempts (Loginizer)
ℹ

Classic Editor ℹ

wpCentral - Manage Multiple
WordPress ℹ

Check the box next to **"Limit Login Attempts"**. This is another layer of protection against hackers.

When Wordpress 5 was released, WordPress changed the default editor (that you use to write your content) to a "page builder" called Gutenberg. A lot of people prefer to use the original (or "classic") editor. The Classic Editor plugin gives you the option of using that original editor if you want to. My advice is to leave this unchecked for now, as you can install it at a later date if you want to check it out.

Leave wpCentral unchecked.

Click the plus sign next to the **"Advanced Options"** title:

■ Advanced Options

Database Name
Type the name of the database to
be created for the installation

Table Prefix

Auto Upgrade ℹ
⦿ Do not Auto Upgrade
◯ Upgrade to **Minor** versions only
◯ Upgrade to any latest version available (**Major** as well as **Minor**)

Auto Upgrade WordPress
Plugins ℹ

Auto Upgrade WordPress
Themes ℹ

Install

The Database Name is set to a random value. You can change this if you want to. I personally have a lot of databases within my own hosting accounts, so prefer to use a name that reminds me of its use. E.g. I might use something like wphar22. The wp prefix would tell me it is a WordPress site, and "har" would tell me which site. The 22 at the end is just a random couple of digits to make the name more difficult to guess.

The table prefix should also be random. Some WordPress installation scripts will use wp_ by default, but hackers know this, and you should avoid it. Choose something random. Softaculous does generate a random prefix, so you can use the default one chosen by the installation routine if you want to.

We then have some auto-upgrade options. If you want WordPress, plugins, and themes to automatically upgrade when new versions are available, check these options. For plugins and themes, I think it is a good idea. However, I would recommend you only set WordPress to auto-upgrade on minor versions. Major version updates can sometimes cause conflicts, so I prefer to do those manually when they happen.

Finally, click the install button. Your WordPress login details will be emailed to you at this address when WordPress is installed.

OK, once the installation has finished, you'll be shown something like this:

Congratulations, the software was installed successfully

WordPress has been successfully installed at :
https://harlunlimited.com
Administrative URL : https://harlunlimited.com/wp-admin/

We hope the installation process was easy.

The first link will load your website (currently a skeleton site created by WordPress).

The second URL listed is the Administrative URL. You can click that link to log in to the WordPress Dashboard for your site. The username and password are those that you used when filling in the Admin Details a few minutes ago. Make sure you bookmark this admin URL.

Go Check Out Your Site

Go and look at your website in a web browser by typing the domain URL into the address bar, or simply clicking the link provided on completion of the installation.

You should see your WordPress site up and running. Of course, it won't have any of your content yet and it does come pre-installed with a few web pages you'll need to delete, but you should see the homepage displaying a "Hello World!" post.

Before we start learning how to configure the site, let's just log in, and then log out again, so we know how.

You should have already bookmarked the login URL, but if not, just add **/wp-admin** (or **wp-login.php**) to the end of the URL, e.g.

http://mydomain.com/wp-admin

You'll be taken to the login screen:

Enter the username and password you chose when you were installing WordPress then click the "Log In" button.

I also recommend you check the "Remember Me" box so that your username and password will be automatically entered next time you log in to your Dashboard.

NOTE: If you ever forget your password, you can click the link under the login boxes to reset your password. The reset instructions will be sent to your admin email address (that's the one you entered when installing WordPress).

After logging in, you'll find yourself inside the Dashboard. You can have a look around but don't go changing anything just yet. Don't worry if it looks a little daunting in there. We'll take a tour of the Dashboard and I'll show you step-by-step, with screenshots, how to set it all up so you can have a great looking website.

Inside the Dashboard, you may have notifications telling you of some plugins or themes (and even WordPress itself) that need updating. We'll do that in a moment. For now, let's log out so you are clear on how to do that.

Move your mouse over the top right where it says "Howdy, Yourname". A menu will appear:

Click the "Log Out" link.

You'll be logged out and taken back to the login screen.

Great, WordPress is installed and you know how to log in and out of the Dashboard.

Tasks to Complete

1. Install WordPress.
2. Log in, have a quick look around the Dashboard, then log out.

WordPress Web Pages

Before we start delving into the inner workings of WordPress and build our own site, I need to talk for a moment about web pages, because WordPress does things in a way that confuses a lot of people. And it is not just beginners that can get confused. Professional web designers that move to WordPress from other platforms can also struggle with this. So, let's start at the beginning...

Websites are made up of web pages. You can think of a web page as a single page of content.

When you want to add a piece of content to your website, e.g. an article, contact form, etc, you need to create a web page to put it on. In WordPress, there are two ways we can create a web page. We can use a WordPress **POST** or a WordPress **PAGE**. I'll go into the differences between these two types of web page later. For now, just realize that these two options exist.

To complicate matters further, WordPress will create some web pages all by itself, to help organize your content.

With a WordPress website, you'll have a homepage, some web pages you create, and some web pages that WordPress creates.

Here is a simplified diagram to help explain the organization of a WordPress website:

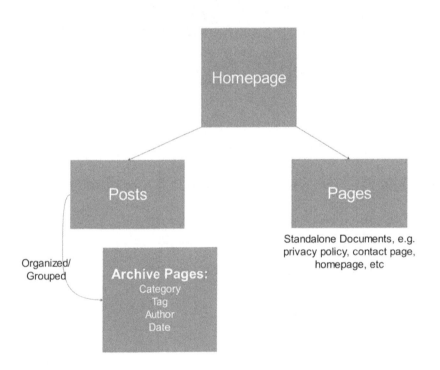

The homepage is a very special page on any website. It can often rank highly in the search engines and can be used to introduce your site to new visitors, guiding them around the website.

We've then got the two types of web pages. Those created with WordPress **posts**, and those created with WordPress **pages**.

Let's start off with pages. These are pretty much standalone pieces of content that are largely unrelated to any other piece of content on the site. A typical use for pages includes "Privacy Policy", "Terms", "Contact Us" and "About Us" pages.

Posts are a completely different beast altogether. If you think about a typical website, you'll often see content organized into "groups" or "categories" on the site. For example, a site on heart health may have several different articles all discussing cholesterol. WordPress "posts" lend themselves to this type of content that needs to be grouped and organized. As you can see in the diagram above, "posts" are organized in a number of different ways.

We will go into a lot of detail on categories and tags as you work through the book, but I want to introduce them here because it illustrates the point I made about WordPress creating pages to organize your content (posts).

You can create something in WordPress called a "category". Posts can then be filed into different categories to organize them. When you create a category, WordPress will automatically create a "category page". A category page is simply a page that lists all posts in the category.

You can also create something in WordPress called a "tag". You can think of tags as very important "keywords" that are related to your post. WordPress will create a "tag page" for every tag you create. These tag pages simply list all posts that have been given that tag. Tags are another way that posts are organized on your site.

As you create posts, WordPress will also create author and date archives. An author archive is a page that lists all posts by an author. Can you guess what a date archive is? Yup. It's a page that lists all posts made on a particular date.

As you can see, WordPress is working in the background, creating multiple pages to help organize the content on your website.

Pre-Installed WordPress Themes

Before we continue, I need to mention something very important.

WordPress uses something called a theme to control the layout, color, fonts, and general design of your site. We will look at these later. What you need to know now is that WordPress pre-installs a few themes to get you started, and sets one of them as default. The theme itself doesn't affect the core functionality of WordPress. It is only there to define the layout of your web pages. Understand that whatever theme you use, you'll still be able to follow 100% of this book, so don't start fretting about this.

Every year or so, WordPress releases a new default theme. Think of these themes as demo themes, as you probably won't want to use them on your final website.

At the time of writing, the last new theme released by WordPress was the Twenty Twenty theme, released on the 12th November 2019. Use the Twenty Twenty theme if you wish, but realize you can actually use any theme you like - there are tens of thousands to choose from. In the past versions of this book, I stuck with the Twenty Sixteen theme because it was easy and intuitive to use. However, some students incorrectly thought the book was not up to date, even saying it used an old version of WordPress. That is incorrect. The theme you use is not related to the version of WordPress you have installed. The theme is simply a "plugin" to WordPress that defines the layout of the web pages. I could use the Twenty Sixteen theme in this book again, but that doesn't mean the WordPress taught in this book is out of date. It simply means I like that theme.

Changing themes is as easy as clicking the mouse button a few times, so don't be afraid to experiment and see what designs are available to suit the topic of your site. Also, be aware that you can change themes at any time in your site's development. Now, before you start. In a year, or ten. Changing themes does not alter the content of your site, just the design of your pages.

So, what theme should you use?

It's important to realize that all themes are a little different. You may see a theme demo online that you like and decide to use that theme on your site. However, to get your site to look like that demo may require installation of plugins and a lot of configuration that only becomes clear after wading through pages of documentation. As someone trying to learn to use Wordpress, you don't need that stress.

My advice is to learn WordPress first, then worry about the theme. After all, you can build out your entire site using any theme, then change it later with a few clicks of the mouse. Choosing a theme now is not a priority (and neither is worrying about plugins).

Once you know how to use WordPress, choosing a theme becomes a lot easier because you'll know your requirements and what to look for. At the moment, while you learn WordPress with this book, the actual theme you use is less important. However, having said that, since all themes are different, I'd highly recommend we all use the same theme. That way my screenshots in this book will match what you are seeing in your WordPress Dashboard.

In this book, I am going to ask you to install a specific free theme to get you started.

I wanted to choose a free theme that was well-established, well-supported, fast-loading, SEO-friendly, and easy to use. Most of all, I wanted to choose a theme that students could see themselves sticking with on completion of this book. A theme that could easily expand to fill their needs. I discounted the Twenty Twenty theme straight away as it does not natively support sidebars (something most people want).

The theme I chose is called Astra.

You can read more about it here:

http://ezseonews.com/astra

There is a free version that will be powerful enough for many users, and a Pro version that adds in even more features. For this book, we'll install and use the free version.

Before we install Astra, let's have a look at the **Themes** section of the Dashboard. If you are not already in your dashboard, make sure you login now.

To view the installed themes (and switch between them), look for the **Appearance** menu on the left, and in the popup menu that appears when you hover your mouse over, select **Themes**.

When the page loads, you'll see the installed themes.

Themes ③ [Add New] [Search installed themes...]

Welcome to the Swedish Museum of Modern Art

Active: Twenty Twenty   Customize

TWENTY SEVENTEEN

Twenty Seventeen

Welcome

Digital strategy for unique small businesses

Twenty Nineteen

+

Add New Theme

The active theme is always the first one on the list. You can see in my screenshot that Twenty Twenty is active.

Each installed theme has a thumbnail hinting at what it will look like on your site.

If you visit your site, you can see what the currently active theme looks like. Let's do that.

In the top-left position of your dashboard, you will see your website name. Place your mouse pointer over the site name and a menu drops down with one item – **Visit Site**. Click the Visit Site link. This will take you to your website as it

appears to anyone that visits.

OK, click the back button on your web browser.

You'll be taken back to the Dashboard, right where you were before clicking on the visit site link.

OK, let's change to another theme.

Move your mouse over one of the other themes installed in your Dashboard and click where it says **Theme Details**. This will open a screen that displays more information about the selected theme. At the bottom, you have two buttons and a delete link.

Activate   Live Preview   Delete

The **Activate** button will make that theme the new active theme.

Go on, try it. Click on Activate.

Once activated, click on the visit site link again to see what your site looks like. It's very different, isn't it?

OK; click the back button in your browser to return to the theme page of the Dashboard.

Check out the third theme in the same way.

During this exercise, I am sure you noticed the **Live Preview** button? You'll have seen it on the

Theme Details screen, but you can also see it if you mouseover an inactive theme:

Clicking **Live Preview** will open a preview screen showing what your site would look like with that theme, but without making it active. Go on, click the **Live Preview** button.

You can make a theme active from the preview screen by clicking the **Activate & Publish** button top left:

If you just want to close the preview screen without activating the theme, click the **X** on the left.

OK, so let's install Astra.

From the **Themes** screen in your dashboard, click the **Add New** button at the top:

On the **Add Themes** screen, enter **Astra** in the search box. The results will be filtered, and you'll see the Astra theme:

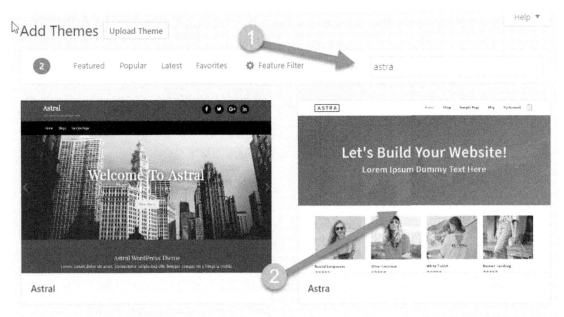

Mouse over the Astra theme and click on the **Install** button:

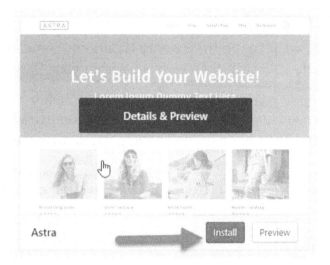

Once the installation is complete, click the **Activate** button:

That's it! Astra is now installed on your site, and being used to define page layouts, colors, fonts, etc. Go and view your site again to see how different it looks.

Delete Un-Used Themes

It is a good idea to delete any themes you are not using for security reasons. Old themes may have security holes that hackers can take advantage of. At the very least, keep all installed themes (yes, even the inactive ones) up to date.

Let's keep Astra as the active theme and delete the other two.

Move your mouse over the Twenty Nineteen theme and click the **Theme Details** button. Click the **Delete** link on the details page. You will be asked for confirmation to delete it.

Repeat the process for the other un-used themes so you are just left with Astra.

Whoops, I've Deleted the Wrong Theme

Maybe you've decided that you want to use the Twenty Nineteen theme after all, but it's gone. The good news is that you can easily re-install themes from within your Dashboard in the same way we installed Astra.

Just go to the **Add Themes** screen and search for the one you want to use, then install and activate it. Go on, try it. Search for the Twenty nineteen theme, but don't install it. That was easy enough to find, wasn't it?

While on the **Add Themes** screen, have a little fun. Click on the **Featured** link at the top to see a list of free featured themes you can install and use.

Have a look at the themes on the **Popular** page.

What about that **Feature Filter** page?

Explore the range of free themes on these pages. Install them if you want, but when you are done, remove them all except Astra.

In the next chapter, we are going to have a look around the WordPress Dashboard.

An Overview of the Dashboard

When you log in to WordPress, you are presented with the Dashboard. This is what it looks like:

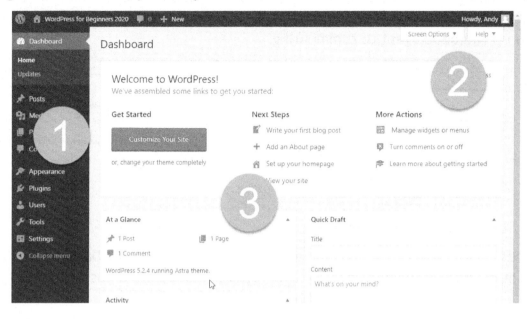

1. The Sidebar
2. Screen Options, Help, Profile & Logout
3. The Main screen

Let's look at each of these in turn.

The Sidebar

The sidebar's purpose is to give you access to the Dashboard navigation menu. This contains all of the tools you need to build, manage and maintain your website. You can add/edit content on your site, upload images, moderate comments, change your site theme, add/remove plugins, and everything else you will need to do as a website owner. We'll look at these features in detail later in the book.

Screen Options, Help, Profile & Logout

Screen Options is a drop-down menu that allows you to decide what is shown on the various screens within the Dashboard. If you click the Screen Options link, you'll see something like this:

What you see will depend on where you are in the dashboard, the version of WordPress you have installed, installed plugins, and themes. These options are context-sensitive and will be relevant to the current page you are viewing. For example, if you are in the section for moderating comments, the screen options will be relevant to commenting.

Columns

☑ Author   ☑ In Response To   ☑ Submitted On

Pagination

Number of items per page: 20

Apply

By changing these options, you can customize what is displayed on your Dashboard. If you don't want to see something, you simply uncheck it. Be aware that not all areas of the dashboard have screen options.

TIP: When following along with this book, if you find something missing from the screen that should be there, go in and check the screen options to ensure that it's enabled.

We will be popping into the screen options a few times in this book.

To the right of the **Screen Options** is a button to access WordPress help. Clicking it opens a help panel:

The left side of this help panel is tabbed, offering you categorized help sections. Like the screen options, the help panel is context-sensitive so it shows you the most useful help items for the Dashboard area you are currently working in (I was in the comments section of my Dashboard when I took this screenshot).

If you need more detailed help, there are links on the right side that take you to the official WordPress documentation and support forums.

Finally, in this area of the Dashboard screen, if you place your mouse over the "Howdy, Yourname" top right, a panel opens:

We saw this earlier in the book.

This menu gives you a direct link to edit your profile (which we will fill out later) and a link to log out of your WordPress Dashboard. Whenever you finish a session in the WordPress Dashboard, it's always a good idea to log out.

The Main Screen

This is where all the work takes place. What you see in the main screen area will depend on where you are in the Dashboard. For example, if you are in the comments section, the main screen area will list all the comments people have made on your site. If you are in the themes section, the main screen will display installed themes, and so on. Some of these screens can be customized using screen options (if available) to show/hide elements.

Tasks to Complete

1. Go in and explore the Dashboard to familiarize yourself with the system.
2. Go and check out the pre-installed WordPress Themes.
3. Install the free version of Astra.
4. Delete all inactive themes, for security reasons.
5. Click on a few of the menu items in the left navigation column and see if screen options are available. If they are, open them up to see what's there. See how the options are related to the page you are viewing in the Dashboard?
6. Have a look at the help options. You won't need any of that now, but it is a good idea to be familiar with these options just in case you get stuck in the future.

Cleaning Out the Pre-Installed Stuff

When you install WordPress, it installs a few default items like the "Hello World" post you saw on the homepage earlier. In addition to that post, there is a "Sample page", a comment, some widgets, and a few plugins.

NOTE: WordPress allows you to create two types of "article" – posts and pages. Don't worry about the differences just yet as we'll look at them later.

In this chapter, we'll look at the pre-installed content, then delete it.

Deleting the "Hello World" Post

If you visit your site homepage, you'll see that the "Hello World" post is displayed front and center.

To delete the post, we need to use the "Posts" menu from the sidebar navigation.

You can either move your mouse over the word **Posts** and select **All Posts** from the popup menu, like this:

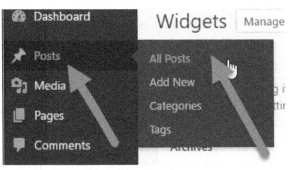

Or you can click the word **Posts** and the sub-menu will become integrated into the left sidebar. At the same time, WordPress will automatically select the first item in the menu – **All Posts:**

This will open a table of all posts on your site:

Something to Try...

Open the **Screen Options** top right, and uncheck/check some of the boxes to see how it affects what you see on your screen. Try out the **Excerpt View** in the **View Mode** section of the screen options (hint: You will need to click the **Apply** button for that to take effect).

OK; now you've had some fun, let's delete the Hello World post.

Move your mouse over the title of the post. A menu appears underneath:

This menu allows you to:

1. Edit the post – Go to the full edit screen with the post loaded for editing.
2. Quick Edit - which allows you to edit some details of the post, but not all. Click it to see the quick edit panel. You can click the **Update** or **Cancel** button to close it when you are done.
3. Trash (or bin, depending on the version of English your WordPress is using) - i.e. delete it.
4. View – which will open the post in the current browser window.

We want to delete the post, so click on the bin/trash link. The screen will refresh, and the post will be gone.

If you accidentally delete a post, don't worry. It will remain in the trash until you empty the trash. I actually want to keep the "Hello World!" post on my site so that I can use it later in the book, so let's undelete the post.

To do this, go to the **All Posts** screen (which is where we are right now) and look for the **Trash** link above the table of posts.

There is a (1) next to it. That means there is one item in the trash (my "Hello World" post). If you click on the link, you'll be taken to the trash where you can see all the posts that were sent there.

If you mouse-over the post title, you'll get another popup menu. This one allows you to restore the post (i.e. undelete it), or delete it permanently.

If you have a lot of posts in the trash and you want to delete them all, click the **Empty Trash** button at the bottom.

NOTE: When WordPress created the "Hello World!" post, it also added a demo comment to the post. When you deleted the post, the comment was also deleted because it belonged to that post. When you undelete (restore) a post, any comments that were deleted with the post are also restored.

I am going to click on the **Restore** link to undelete the Hello World post and comment. You can do the same if you wish. You know how to delete it when you decide you want to.

Deleting the Sample Page

In the sidebar navigation of your Dashboard, open the **Pages** menu and click on **All Pages**.

Like the posts section, this will bring up a list of all pages on the site. There will probably be two:

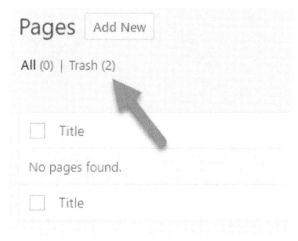

Mouseover each page title in turn, and click the **Trash** link underneath it.

As with posts, pages remain in the trash until it's emptied, so they too can be restored if required.

Deleting Widgets

WordPress pre-configured your website with a number of widgets. A widget is simply a "feature" that you can add to your website in predefined areas of the page, e.g. the sidebar, footer, etc. You can see them if you look at your website:

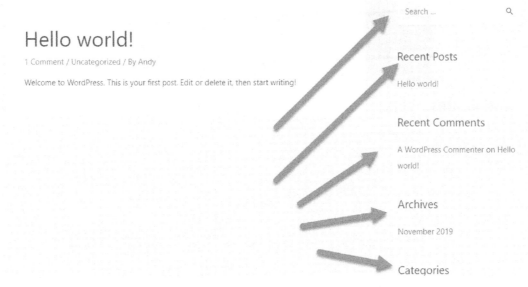

Those are widgets on the right.

There are five in that screenshot. The first widget adds a search box. The second adds a list of recent posts. The third shows the recent comments on the site. The fourth shows post archives. The bottom one is cut off but would list the categories of posts on the site.

Let's explore the widgetized areas, then delete those widgets.

In your Dashboard, move your mouse over the **Appearance** menu, and click on **Widgets**:

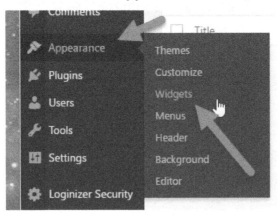

This will take you to the widget screen:

The screen is split into two sections.

On the left, you'll see the **Available Widgets**.

On the right, you have "widgetized areas". These are areas on your web page that can hold widgets.

For example, the top widgetized area in that screenshot is the **Sidebar**. If I click the small down arrow in the sidebar box, it will open up and show what widgets are configured in the sidebar:

You can see the five widgets we saw previously at the top of the sidebar. Any widgets in this area will appear in the sidebar on the website. This sidebar currently has 6 widgets.

You can insert widgets into the widgetized areas of your site by dragging and dropping them from the left side of the screen, onto the corresponding area on the right. Be aware that different themes have different widgetized areas, so if you are not using the Astra theme, you will be seeing something a little different on the right-hand side.

The Astra theme has other areas besides the sidebar. These correspond to areas on your web pages that can accept widgets. In Astra, the sidebar is the only active area by default, though the other areas can be turned on. Astra tends to keep features turned off until required. That helps speed up the page load times which can only be good for SEO.

Although all WordPress themes are different, common widget areas include the footer, sidebar, and header of the web page.

We'll look at widgets and widgetized areas in more detail later.

Let's clear out the pre-installed widgets.

On the widgets screen, open the "Main Sidebar" area by clicking the small downward pointing arrow.

You'll see the six widgets installed by WordPress.

Each widget has a small downward-pointing arrow next to it on the right. Click this arrow to open the settings for that particular widget. Here are the recent post widget settings:

You can enter a title (leaving this blank will use the default title for the widget, in this case, "Recent Posts"). You can also specify how many posts to show. This one is set to 5.

To delete the widget, click the **Delete** link bottom left.

The widget will disappear from the Main Sidebar area. Repeat to delete all other widgets in the sidebar. The only one I am leaving for now is the **Meta** widget. This gives me an easy link to log in to my site from the homepage, so I'll keep it there for now while I am working on the site. You can do the same if you wish.

OK, we are done cleaning out WordPress.

Go and visit your site:

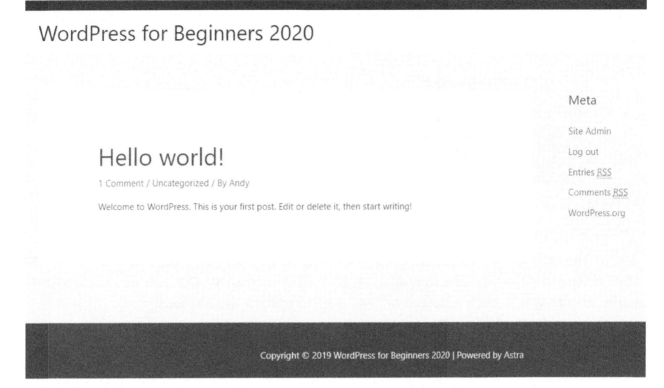

If you deleted the Hello World post, you will just see a message saying, "Nothing Found". In my screenshot, the Hello World post is shown on the homepage, and you can see the Meta widget I left in the right sidebar.

Tasks to Complete

1. Delete the Hello World post and then restore it.
2. Delete the pre-installed Page.
3. Explore the various widgets that WordPress has given you. Drag & drop them into the main sidebar to see what they look like on your website. Note that some widgets may show nothing at all until there is some content for the widget to work with.

Dashboard Updates

WordPress makes it easy for us to know when there are updates. It shows a number in a red circle next to the **Updates** menu. That number tells you how many updates are available. On this website, there are 11!

Available updates can include plugins, themes and WordPress itself!

Click on the **Updates** menu item.

At the top of the screen, you'll see a notification whenever there is a new update to WordPress itself. Click on the **Update Now** link to update WordPress if necessary. Occasionally these WordPress updates will require you to click a button or two, e.g. to update the database:

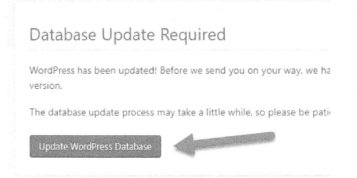

Just follow all screen prompts, and the update will complete and take you back to the Dashboard.

Back on the **Updates** screen, WordPress will be up-to-date but there may be plugins that need updating. On my site, there are ten that need updating:

Plugins

The following plugins have new versions available. Check the ones you want to update and then click "Update

Update Plugins

Select All

All In One WP Security
You have version 4.3.3.1 installed. Update to 4.4.2. View version 4.4.2 details.
Compatibility with WordPress 5.2.4: 100% (according to its author)

Contact Form 7
You have version 5.0.1 installed. Update to 5.1.4. View version 5.1.4 details.
Compatibility with WordPress 5.2.4: 100% (according to its author)

Cookie Consent
You have version 2.3.10 installed. Update to 2.3.15. View version 2.3.15 details.
Compatibility with WordPress 5.2.4: Unknown

Google XML Sitemaps
You have version 4.0.9 installed. Update to 4.1.0. View version 4.1.0 details.
Compatibility with WordPress 5.2.4: 100% (according to its author)

LiteSpeed Cache
You have version 2.2.5 installed. Update to 2.9.9. View version 2.9.9 details.

You can update all the plugins by checking the boxes next to each one (the **Select All** checkbox will check them all with a single click), and then click the **Update Plugins** button.

Once the plugin updates have been completed, WordPress will ask you where you want to go next:

All updates have been completed.

Return to Plugins page | Return to WordPress Updates page

If there are still updates to perform, click the link to return to WordPress updates.

If there are no more updates available, you can click on any of the sidebar menus to go wherever you want.

In the next chapter, we will configure WordPress so that it is ready for our content.

Tasks to Complete

1. Check to see if there are any updates needing your attention. If there are, go and update everything. Whenever you log in to your Dashboard, if there are updates pending, it is a good idea (for security reasons) to update them immediately.

WordPress Settings

In the sidebar, you'll see an item labeled **Settings**.

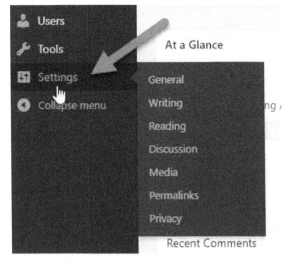

Within **Settings,** there are a number of items.

Important: Themes and plugins can add items to the sidebar menu system. If you have items in your menu that are not shown in this book, chances are they have been added by a plugin or theme you installed. The menu system I am going to show you is the core WordPress menu, with no plugins installed, and two themes – Astra and Twenty Twenty (I'll tell you why I kept this theme later in this section).

Let's look at each one in turn and configure things as we go through.

General Settings

The General settings page defines some of the basic website settings.

At the top of the screen, the first few settings look like this:

General Settings

Site Title	WordPress for Beginners 2020
Tagline	Just another WordPress site
	In a few words, explain what this site is about.
WordPress Address (URL)	http://wordpress-for-beginners-2020.local
Site Address (URL)	http://wordpress-for-beginners-2020.local
	Enter the address here if you want your site home page to be different from your WordPress installation directory.
Administration Email Address	dev-email@flywheel.local
	This address is used for admin purposes. If you change this we will send you an email at your new address to confirm it. The new address will not become active until confirmed.

The information on the General Settings page was filled in when you installed WordPress, and there is probably no reason to change anything.

Right at the top is the Site Title. This is usually the same as the domain name but doesn't have to be.

Under the title is the Tagline. On some themes, the tagline is displayed in the site header, right under the site name.

You can use the tagline to give your visitors more information about your website. A tagline might be your website's "catchphrase", slogan, mission statement, or just a very brief, one-sentence description.

The next two fields on this settings page are the **WordPress Address (URL)** and the **Site Address (URL)**. The WordPress Address is the URL where WordPress is installed, and the Site Address is the URL you go to view the site in a browser. Since we installed it in the root folder of this site, the WordPress Address is identical to the Site Address.

NOTE: Advanced users might want to install WordPress in a folder on their server, yet still have the site appear as if it were in the root folder. They can achieve this by using the WordPress Address (URL) field. Confused? Don't be. We won't be doing this.

Next on this setting page is the email address. This is very important as you'll get all "admin" notifications sent to this email address. Make sure you use a valid email that you check frequently.

Lower down this General Setting page are these options:

Membership	☐ Anyone can register
New User Default Role	Subscriber ▼

The **Membership** option allows visitors to sign up on your site, with their role being defined in the **New User Default Role** drop-down box.

E.g. you could allow visitors to sign up as subscribers or maybe contributors to your site. This can open up a whole can of security worms, so I don't advise you enable this option. If you want to create a "membership" site, use a dedicated, secure WordPress membership plugin like Wishlist Member (which can turn any WordPress site into a fully-fledged membership site).

The rest of the settings on this page allow you to set your time zone, date and time formats.

The timezone is used to correctly timestamp posts on your site. Since we'll look at how you can schedule your posts into the future, the correct time zone will ensure your posts are going out on the intended dates and times.

Select the date and time format you use.

You can also set the day you use for the start of the week. This will be used if you use a calendar widget in your sidebar. If you choose Monday as the start of the week, then Monday will be the first column in the calendar.

If you make any changes to the settings on the General Settings tab, make sure you save the changes when you are finished.

Writing

In the **Settings** menu, click on **Writing**.

The writing settings control the user interface you see when you are adding/editing posts. Let's look at the options.

Here are the first two:

Writing Settings

Default Post Category	Uncategorised ▼
Default Post Format	Standard ▼

The **Default Post Category** is the category that a post will be assigned to if you don't manually select a category. We haven't set up any categories yet. WordPress set one up for us during installation, called **Uncategorized**, so that is the current default. We'll rename that to something more useful when we look at categories later in the book.

The **Default Post Format** is the default layout/appearance of the posts you add to your site. Different themes will have different post formats you can use. In Astra, here are your options:

Default Post Format Standard ▼

Standard
Aside
Chat
Gallery
Link
Image
Quote
Status
Video
Audio

Each of these formats will modify how that post looks, so I recommend you use the Standard option for the default value, and then change the format on a post by post basis if needed. I should point out that I rarely change from the default "Standard".

Here are the next few settings:

The Post via e-mail can be set up so that you can post content to your site by sending it in as an email. This is beyond the scope of this book.

The final setting on this page is important. It's the update services:

Update Services

When you publish a new post, WordPress automatically notifies the follow
Codex. Separate multiple service URLs with line breaks.

    http://rpc.pingomatic.com/

Save Changes

If you see this:

Update Services

WordPress is not notifying any Update Services because of your site's visibility settings.

.. then you have checked the **"Search Engine Visibility"** box in the Reading settings. We'll cover that in a moment.

Basically, every time you post new content on your site, a message is sent to all "services" in this list (currently just one) to let them know there is new content. They will then typically come over to your site to index the content.

This list helps your content get noticed and included more quickly in the search engines. WordPress installs just one service, but I recommend you add more.

Do a search on Google for "WordPress Ping List" and you'll find ready-made lists created by other webmasters. Just find a list and paste it into the box. Save your changes before moving to the next settings page.

Reading

In the **Settings** menu, click **Reading**.

The reading settings define how your visitors will see certain aspects of your site.

There are only a few settings here, but they are important.

Reading Settings

Blog pages show at most	10 posts
Syndication feeds show the most recent	10 items
For each article in a feed, show	⦿ Full text ◯ Summary
Search Engine Visibility	☐ Discourage search engines from indexing this site *It is up to search engines to honor this request.*

Save Changes

Some pages on your site like the category, tag, and homepage, can show lists of posts. **Blog pages show at most**, defines how many posts appear on those pages.

Keeping the default settings shown in the screenshot above, here is an example. If you have a category on your site called "types of roses", WordPress will create a category page called "Types of Roses". That page will list all posts in that category. If you have 15 articles, each describing a different rose, then WordPress will create two category pages to hold those articles. The first category page will have links to the first 10, and the second will list the remaining 5.

I recommend you leave the setting at the default 10.

Syndication feeds show the most recent, refers to your website's RSS feed. Every WordPress site has an RSS feed (in fact it has many RSS feeds). An RSS feed is just a list of the most recent posts with a link and a description of each post. This setting allows you to define how many of your most recent posts appear in the feed. Again, I recommend 10. We'll look at RSS feeds in more detail later.

For each article in a feed, show, defines what content is shown in the feed. If you select "Full Text", then the complete content of each post is included in the feed. This can make your feed very long, and also give spammers a chance to steal your content with tools designed to scrape RSS feeds and post the content to their own sites.

I recommend you change this setting to "Summary". That way only a short summary of each post will be displayed in the feed, which is far less appealing to spammers and easier on the eye for those who genuinely follow your active RSS feeds.

Search Engine Visibility allows you to effectively hide your site from the search engines. If you are working on a site that you don't want the search engines to find, you can check this box. Note that if you check this box, you effectively switch off the Update Services section in the writing settings.

I allow search engines to visit and index my site from day 1. Yes, the search engines will find content that is not finished, but that's OK because they'll come back and check the site periodically to pick up changes.

Whether you block the search engines now or not is up to you. Just remember that if you do, your site won't start appearing in the search engines until you unblock them.

I recommend you leave this setting unchecked.

Make sure you click the **Save Changes** button at the bottom if you've edited the settings on the screen.

NOTE: If you have skipped ahead and created a WordPress "Page" there will be another section at the top of these settings which defines what is displayed on the homepage:

Reading Settings

Your homepage displays	● Your latest posts
	○ A static page (select below)
Homepage:	— Select — ▾
Posts page:	— Select — ▾

The default setting is **Your Latest Posts**. This will display the most recent posts on your homepage. The number of posts displayed on your homepage is determined by whatever you have "Blog pages show at most" set to. Since the default is 10, your last 10 posts will appear on your homepage.

It is possible to set up the homepage like a more traditional website, with a single article forming the basis of the homepage content. You can do this in WordPress by creating a WordPress PAGE that contains your homepage article. You then select **A Static Page** from the options above and choose the page from the **Homepage** drop-down list. We'll do this later.

Discussion

In the **Settings** menu, click **Discussion**.

The discussion settings are related to comments that visitors may leave at the end of your posts. There are a few settings we need to change from the default.

Here are the first few settings in the discussion options:

Default article settings

☑ Attempt to notify any blogs linked to from the article

☑ Allow link notifications from other blogs (pingbacks and trackbacks) on new articles

☑ Allow people to post comments on new articles

(These settings may be overridden for Individual articles.)

Attempt to notify any blogs linked to from the article should be left checked. Whenever you write an article and link to another site, WordPress will try to notify that site that you have linked to them. WordPress does this by sending what is called a Ping. Pings will show up in the comment system of the receiving blog and can be approved like a comment. If it is approved, that "pingback" will appear near the comments section on that blog, giving you a link back to your site.

NOTE: Any website can turn pingbacks off. If a ping is sent to a site where pingbacks are OFF, then it won't appear in their comment system.

Here are some example pingbacks published on a web page:

3 Responses to *Men's Health Week Proclamations*

1. Pingback: health » Blog Archive » Focus on Men's Health Week This Father's Day : Healthymagination

2. Pingback: Focus on Men's Health Week This Father's Day : Healthymagination – health

3. Pingback: Focus on Men's Health Week This Father's Day : Healthymagination – men health

Each pingback is a link back to a website that has linked to this webpage.

The next option - **Allow link notifications from other blogs (pingbacks and trackbacks)** allows you to turn pingbacks and trackbacks (trackbacks are very similar to pingbacks) off. If you uncheck this, you will not receive pingbacks or trackbacks.

Should you check it or not?

Well, it's always nice to see when a site is linking to your content. However, there is a technique used by spammers to send fake trackbacks & pingbacks to your site. They are trying to get you to approve their trackback so that your site will then link to theirs.

Personally, I uncheck this option, but if you do leave it checked, I recommend you never approve a trackback or pingback. They are nearly always spam!

Allow people to post comments on new articles should remain checked. It is important that you let your visitors comment on your site's content. A lot of people disable this because they think moderating comments is too much work, but from an SEO point of view, search engines love to see active discussions on websites. Leave it checked!

The next section of options is shown below:

Other comment settings
- ☑ Comment author must fill out name and email
- ☐ Users must be registered and logged in to comment
- ☐ Automatically close comments on articles older than 14 days
- ☑ Show comments cookies opt-in checkbox, allowing comment author cookies to be set.
- ☑ Enable threaded (nested) comments 5 ▾ levels deep
- ☐ Break comments into pages with 50 top level comments per page and the last ▾ page displayed by default

Comments should be displayed with the older ▾ comments at the top of each page

Leave these at their default value (shown above).

The options are self-explanatory but let's go through them quickly.

The first option requires commenters to fill in a name and email. This is very important and often a good indicator of legitimate/spam comments. Spammers tend to fill the name field with keywords (for SEO purposes), whereas legitimate commenters are more likely to use a real name. The email is nice too, so you can follow up with commenters.

The second item should remain unchecked because we probably do not allow visitors to register and login to our site. We do want *all* visitors to have the option of leaving a comment though.

The third option allows you to close the comment sections on posts after a certain number of days. I like to leave comments open indefinitely as you never know when someone will find your article and want to have their say. However, if you want to cut back on spam comments, then close comments after a reasonable length of time, say 30 days.

The option to **Show comments cookies opt-in checkbox** is for GDPR compliance and should remain checked if you have any visitors coming from the EU. When checked, a checkbox appears at the bottom of the comment form (on a post), which gives your visitors the option of saving their name, email, and website information in their browser, so it can be used the next time they comment.

☐ Save my name, email, and website in this browser for the next time I comment.

POST COMMENT

Note that you won't see this if you are logged into your dashboard. If you want to see it, visit your hello world post in an incognito browser window.

Nested comments should be enabled. This allows people to engage in discussions within the comments section, with replies to previous comments "nested" underneath the comment they are replying to. Here is an example showing how nested comments appear on my site:

Marshall says:
18/6/2013 at 06:06

I purchased the KD Suite tonight because Andy does good videos. I could have purchased directly from Guindon since I had purchased other products from him. However the productpay.com fulfillment system absolutely sucks. I did not get my bonus downloads because the bonus page got closed before I could get all the membership BS set up and then back to the download page. As opposed to other systems such as JVZoo where you get download information and login information from them, productpay sucks your money and does not much else. And they have no way to contact them without setting up another account with them just to send a support ticket. Plus they hide behind Domains by Proxy owned by Godaddy.com. What kind of legitimate fulfillment company needs to hide their registration information. I have contacted Guindon directly about this and I am sure Dave will make it right. But what a pain in the butt process. If you purchase from productpay.com just be forwarned to download everything first then worry about any membership BS.

You can bet none of Dr Andy's membership sites worked like this. I know because I bought a lot of his products.

Reply

Andy Williams says:
18/6/2013 at 07:59

Totally agree Marshall. They really could do a lot better. Also, thanks for your loyalty 😊

Reply

Marshall says:
18/6/2013 at 09:56

Andy You are welcome. Your software has always worked out of the box without a lot of bugs. And the very few that came up you fixed right away. Your courses were right on the mark too. For what it is worth, Dave got about 5 emails from me tonight so maybe he will rethink his choice of fulfillment companies.

The KD Bestseller analyzer was worth the hassle of getting it and getting it activated. I have played with it for about 3 hours tonight. My niche I was writing in is a real loser for making money. The fiction adventure, romance are really hot now. I have one more herb book to do

You can see that replies to the previous comment are nested underneath, making it clear that the comments are part of a conversation.

The last two options in this section relate to how comments are displayed on the page. If you want, comments can be spread across multiple pages, with say 50 comments per page (default). However, I leave this option unchecked so that all comments for an article appear on the same page. If you find that you get hundreds of comments per article (which will slow down the load time of the page), you might want to enable this option so pages load faster.

The final option in this section allows you to choose whether you want older or newer comments at the top of the comments section.

I prefer comments listed in the order in which they are submitted, as that makes more sense to me. Therefore, I'd leave the setting as "older".

The next section of these settings is shown below:

Email me whenever	✓ Anyone posts a comment
	✓ A comment is held for moderation
Before a comment appears	✓ Comment must be manually approved
	☐ Comment author must have a previously approved comment

You can choose to be notified via email when someone posts a comment, and/or when a comment is held for moderation. The way I suggest you set up your site is that all comments are held for moderation, so effectively, those two options are the same thing.

Check one or other of these two options so you know when there are comments waiting for approval. When you get an email notification, you can then log in to your Dashboard and either approve the comment (so it goes live on your site) or send it to trash if it's blatant spam.

The second two options shown above relate to when a comment can appear on the site. Check the box next to **Comment must be manually approved**. This will mean ALL comments must be approved by you before appearing on the site.

The second option will allow you to auto-approve comments by commenters that have had previous comments approved (i.e. trusted commenters). I recommend you leave this option unchecked for reasons I will explain in a moment. If you did want to use this feature, the first option would need to be unchecked.

So why do I not recommend this option?

A hacking technique (zero-day exploit) targeted sites that were set up to auto-approve comments once a first comment was approved. Hackers would get a harmless comment approved, and then post a comment that contained malicious JavaScript. The JavaScript comment would never be manually approved on its own, but with the first comment already approved, it would get automatic approval.

The comment moderation settings are not important to us since all comments will be moderated.

Comment Moderation	Hold a comment in the queue if it contains 2 or more links. (A common characteristic of comment spam is a large number of hyperlinks.)
	When a comment contains any of these words in its content, name, URL, email, or IP, it will be held in the moderation queue. One word or IP per line. It will match inside words, so "press" will match "WordPress".

If you do not want to manually moderate all comments, you can use these settings to automatically add a comment to the moderation queue IF it has a certain number of links in it (default is 2), OR the comment contains a word that is listed in the big box.

The Comment Blacklist box allows you to set up a blacklist to automatically reject comments.

Comment Blacklist	When a comment contains any of these words in its content, name, URL, email, or IP, it will be put in the trash. One word or IP per line. It will match inside words, so "press" will match "WordPress".

Essentially any comment that contains a word or URL listed in this box, or comes from an email address or IP address listed in this box, will automatically be sent to the trash.

That means you can set up your blacklist with "unsavory" words, email addresses, URLs or IP addresses of known spammers, and you'll never see those comments in your moderation queue. The comment blacklist can significantly cut down on your comment moderation, so I suggest you do a search on Google for **WordPress comment blacklist** and use a list that someone else has already put together (you'll find a few). Just copy and paste their list into the box and save the settings.

The final section of the discussion options is related to Avatars:

Avatars

An avatar is an image that follows you from weblog to weblog appearing beside your name when you comment on ava Here you can enable the display of avatars for people who comment on your site.

Avatar Display	☑ Show Avatars
Maximum Rating	⦿ G — Suitable for all audiences
	◯ PG — Possibly offensive, usually for audiences 13 and above
	◯ R — Intended for adult audiences above 17
	◯ X — Even more mature than above

An Avatar is an image/photo that can appear next to the commenter's name if they have set up something called a Gravatar (which we will revisit later).

I think it is nice to see who is leaving comments, so I recommend you leave Avatars on (first setting).

For most websites, you should have the maximum rating set to G. This will then hide any Avatars that are not suitable for your viewers. Avatars are assigned ratings when you create them over at Gravatar.com, so this rating system is only as good as the honesty of the person creating the avatar.

The final setting allows you to define the default action if someone does not have an Avatar set up for their email address.

For users without a custom avatar of their own, you can either display a generated one based on their email address.

- ○ Mystery Person
- ◉ Blank ←
- ○ Gravatar Logo
- ○ Identicon (Generated)
- ○ Wavatar (Generated)
- ○ MonsterID (Generated)
- ○ Retro (Generated)

I personally select **Blank** so that no avatar is shown as I think it looks better than one with a load of "mystery person" (or other) generated avatars.

When you have finished with these settings, save the changes.

Media

Click on the **Media** link in the **Settings** menu.

The media settings relate to images and other media that you might insert into your site.

Image sizes

The sizes listed below determine the maximum dimensions in pixels to use when adding an image to the

Thumbnail size	Width 150 Height 150
	☑ Crop thumbnail to exact dimensions (normally thumbnail
Medium size	Max Width 300 Max Height 300
Large size	Max Width 1024 Max Height 1024

These first few settings allow you to define the maximum dimensions for the thumbnail, medium, and large images. You can leave these at their default settings.

The final option asks whether you want your uploaded images to be organized into month- and year-based folders.

Uploading Files

☑ Organize my uploads into month- and year-based folders

Save Changes

I'd recommend you leave this checked, just so your images are organized into dates on your server. This can help you find the images later if you need to.

Permalinks

Click on the **Permalinks** item in the **Settings** menu.

The Permalink settings define how the URLs (web addresses) are structured for the web pages on your site.

We want the URLs on our site to help visitors and search engines, so I recommend they contain both the category and filename:

Select the **Custom Structure** radio button at the bottom of the list and clear any tags from the white box.

To create the desired URL structure, click on the **%category%** button, followed by the **%postname%** button:

Watch how the permalink structure is automatically written as your custom structure.

Save the changes.

The URLs on your site will now look like this:

http://mydomain.com/category/post-name

You'll see why this makes so much sense when you start adding posts to your website.

The last two options on this settings page are shown below:

Optional

If you like, you may enter custom structures for your category and tag URLs here. For example, using t‹ would make your category links like `http://harlun.co.uk/topics/uncategorized/` . If you leave t used.

Category base

Tag base

Save Changes

I would leave these two boxes empty.

When WordPress creates a category page or a tag page, the URL will include the word "category" or "tag" to tell you that you are on a special type of web page.

For example:

http://mydomain.com/**category**/roses/

.. might be the URL of a category page listing posts about Roses, and

http://mydomain.com/**tag**/red

.. might be a tag page listing all posts about red roses on the site (i.e. posts that were tagged with the word "red").

These words in the URL help identify the type of page as a category or tag page. That is useful to search engines and visitors.

If you enter a word into the category base or tag base, the URLs will contain the words you enter here, rather than the default "category" or "tag".

Having keywords in your URL can be helpful, BUT, with Google on the warpath against web spammers, I would not even consider entering a category base or tag base. Leave those boxes empty.

Privacy

Finally, click on the **Privacy** link in the **Settings** menu.

The Privacy settings were introduced to help website owners get ready for GDPR compliance. If you don't know what that is, I recommend you research it a little. It is essentially a privacy law. One of the first steps in becoming compliant is to have a good privacy policy that visitors can read. This will tell them what information if any, your site collects and stores.

The Privacy options allow you to select an existing privacy policy if you already have one, or create a new one. When we cleared out pre-installed pages, we deleted a draft privacy policy created by WordPress. Go and restore that one if you want, or create a new one by clicking on the **Create New Page** button. WordPress will create a new draft policy for you that you can then edit and update.

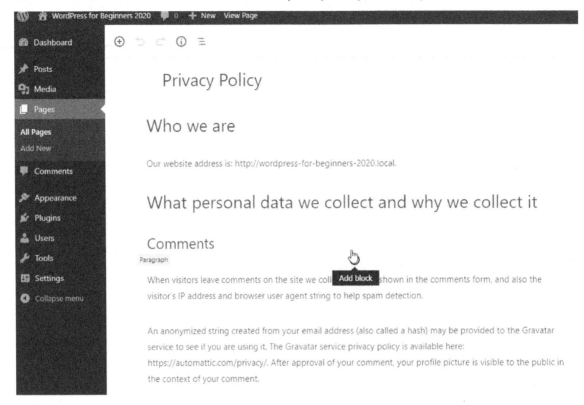

WordPress will include essential information relating to WordPress itself, but you will need to go through the policy and flesh it out. Once it is complete, save the policy. On the Privacy settings page, make sure your new privacy policy is selected:

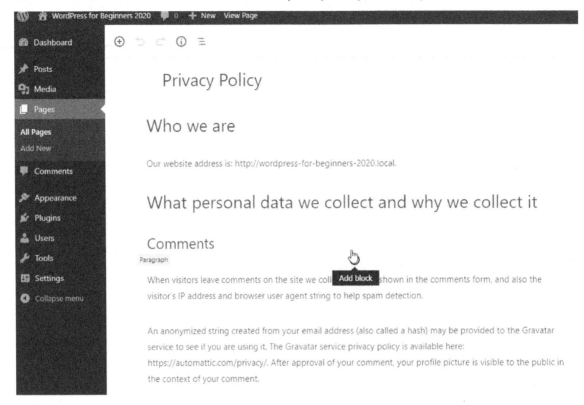

This chapter has hopefully given you a better understanding of the **Settings** menu, how it is organized, and what the important settings do.

Congratulations!

You have now set up WordPress ready for your own content.

Tasks to Complete

1. Go through each of the items inside the settings menu and make the changes described in this chapter.

RSS Feeds

We mentioned RSS feeds earlier when setting up the Reading options.

RSS feeds are an important part of your WordPress website, so I wanted to spend a little more time on this.

RSS stands for **R**eally **S**imple **S**yndication (or **R**ich **S**ite Summary). An RSS feed lists information about the most recent posts on your site. This information is typically the title of the post (which links to the article on your website), and a description of it, which can be short or the entire piece.

The RSS feed is an XML document that would be difficult to read without special software, but XML is the perfect "language" to store this information.

Here is the raw XML for just the first item in that RSS feed:

```
<title>Juicing for Restless Legs Syndrome</title>
<link>https://juicingtherainbow.com/3659/natural-health/juicing-for-
restless-legs-syndrome/</link>
<comments>https://juicingtherainbow.com/3659/natural-health/juicing-for-
restless-legs-syndrome/#respond</comments>
<pubDate>Tue, 13 Mar 2018 09:31:24 +0000</pubDate>
<dc:creator><![CDATA[Andy Williams]]></dc:creator>
          <category><![CDATA[Natural Health]]></category>

<guid isPermaLink="false">https://juicingtherainbow.com/?p=3659</guid>
<description><![CDATA[<p>Restless Leg Syndrome is like ants crawling
inside the veins of you legs and is will keep you awake at night. There are a number of
reasons for this syndrome, some of them curable.</p>
<p>The post <a rel="nofollow" href="https://juicingtherainbow.com/3659/natural-
health/juicing-for-restless-legs-syndrome/">Juicing for Restless Legs Syndrome</a>
appeared first on <a rel="nofollow" href="https://juicingtherainbow.com">Juicing the
Rainbow</a>.</p>
]]></description>
          <wfw:commentRss>https://juicingtherainbow.com/3659/natural-health/juicing-
for-restless-legs-syndrome/feed/</wfw:commentRss>
<slash:comments>0</slash:comments>
</item>
<item>
```

Every post in the RSS feed has an entry like this.

RSS feeds provide an easy way for people to follow the information they are interested in.

For example, if someone was interested in juicing, they could take the RSS feed from their favorite juicing websites and add them to an RSS reader, like Feedly. Feed readers format the XML feed so it is easy for humans to read it:

Alternative Medicine

FDA Bans Import of Meds From Chinese Firm

♠ 500+   Holistic Medicine: What It Is, Treatment... / 2d

The 'import alert' from the FDA against Zhejiang Huahai Pharmaceuticals comes after a series of recalls for valsartan heart and blood pressure drugs that include ingredients made by ZHP.

The effect of Aloe Vera gel on prevention of pressure ulcers in patients hospitalized in the orthopedic wards: a randomized triple-blind clinical trial

BMC Complementary and Alternative Medici... / 1d

One of the most common orthopedic problems is the incidence of pressure ulcer followed by immobility. This study aimed to investigate the effect of Aloe Vera gel on the prevention of pressure ulcer in patients ho...

Facts You Should Know About This Year's Flu Season

Using a tool like Feedly, you can follow dozens of RSS feeds. RSS used this way allows you to scan hundreds of articles by title and description, and only click through to read the ones that you are really interested in.

That is why we have RSS feeds on our site.

WordPress Has Multiple RSS Feeds

WordPress has the main RSS feed at **mydomain.com/feed**. Type that into your web browser substituting mydomain.com for your real domain name, and you'll see yours. However, WordPress also creates a lot of other RSS feeds.

Remember earlier when we looked at how WordPress created some web pages itself, to help organize your posts? These included category pages, tag pages, author pages and so on. These types of pages are called "archive" pages because they list (or archive) multiple relevant posts. Each archive page has its own RSS feed, created by WordPress, to list all posts within that archive.

For example, an RSS feed is created for each category page on your site. If you have a category called "roses", then there will be an RSS feed showing just the posts in the roses category.

To find the URL of any category page feed, simply go to the category page on the site and add "**/feed**" to the end of it, like this:

```
<title>Juice recipes &#8211; Juicing the Rainbow</title>
<atom:link href="https://juicingtherainbow.com/category/recipes/juice/feed/" rel="self" type="app
<link>https://juicingtherainbow.com</link>
<description>Live, love, juice!</description>
<lastBuildDate>Fri, 10 Aug 2018 11:36:32 +0000</lastBuildDate>
<language>en-US</language>
<sy:updatePeriod>hourly</sy:updatePeriod>
<sy:updateFrequency>1</sy:updateFrequency>
<generator>https://wordpress.org/?v=4.9.8</generator>
<item>
        <title>Fruity Goodness</title>
        <link>https://juicingtherainbow.com/3610/recipes/juice/fruity-goodness/</link>
        <comments>https://juicingtherainbow.com/3610/recipes/juice/fruity-goodness/#respond</comm
        <pubDate>Tue, 17 Jan 2017 10:36:40 +0000</pubDate>
        <dc:creator><![CDATA[Andy Williams]]></dc:creator>
```

Other RSS feeds created by WordPress include RSS feeds for tag pages, author pages, comments, search results, and so on. You can read more about WordPress RSS feeds here if you're interested:

http://codex.WordPress.org/WordPress_Feeds

RSS Feeds Can Help Pages Get Indexed

RSS feeds contain links to the pages on our website. We can use that fact to help our content get found more quickly by the search engines. To do this, we simply need to submit the RSS feed to an RSS directory, like Feedage.com.

Search Google for **RSS feed submission** and you'll find more sites where you can submit your main feed. I recommend only submitting it to 3 or 4 of the top RSS feed directories though.

When you post a new article on your site, the feeds on your site are updated, which in turn updates the feed on the RSS directories. These directories now contain a link back to your new article. The search engines monitor sites like this to find new content, so your new article is found very quickly.

Tasks to Complete

1. Go and have a look at Feedly.com and signup for a free account. Subscribe to some feeds that are of interest and look through them to find articles that appeal to you. This will give you a good idea of how feeds can be helpful.

2. Since you currently have no posts on your site, you won't have any meaningful feeds. Once you have some published posts, go and find the various feed URLs (main feed, category feed, tag feed, author feed & search feed).

User Profile

When someone comes to your website, they often want to see who is behind the information. Your user profile in WordPress allows you to tell your visitors a little bit about yourself.

In the Dashboard, hover your mouse over **Users** in the navigation menu and then select **Your Profile**. Alternatively, you can hover your mouse over the "Howdy, Yourname" in the admin bar at the top of the screen and click on your name, or **Edit My Profile.**

Your user profile will load.

At the top of the Profile screen you'll see a couple of settings:

Personal Options

Visual Editor   ☐ Disable the visual editor when writing

Syntax Highlighting   ☐ Disable syntax highlighting when editing code

Leave these both unchecked, as they disable useful features of the Dashboard. Under these options, you can change the color scheme of the Dashboard if you don't like the default.

Admin Color Scheme   ○ Default   ○ Light   ○ Blue   ○ Coffee

                            ● Ectoplasm   ○ Midnight   ○ Ocean   ○ Sunrise

As you check an option, your Dashboard color scheme will change to reflect your choice. You may be spending a lot of time in your Dashboard, so choose a color scheme you like.

We then have these two options:

Keyboard Shortcuts   ☐ Enable keyboard shortcuts for comment moderation. More information

Toolbar   ☑ Show Toolbar when viewing site

I don't use keyboard shortcuts for comment moderation, but if you'd like to, enable the option and follow the "More Information" link to learn how to use it.

Show Toolbar when viewing site is an important option and should be checked. We will look at that later.

The next set of Profile options are for your name:

Name

Username	Andy
First Name	Andy
Last Name	Williams
Nickname *(required)*	Andy
Display name publicly as	Andy Williams ⌄

Your username cannot be changed. It will be whatever you chose when you installed WordPress.

Enter your real first and last name (or your persona if you are working with a pen name).

For the nickname, you can write anything. I typically use my first name.

The **Display name publicly** field is populated with names built from the

personal information entered on this screen.

First Name	Andy
Last Name	Williams
Nickname *(required)*	AJ
Display name publicly as	Andy ▾
	Andy
	Williams
	Andy Williams
	Williams Andy
Contact Info	AJ
Email *(required)*	

Whatever you choose will be the name used on each page of your website telling the visitors who wrote the article:

Hello world!

1 Comment / Uncategorized / By Andy

Welcome to WordPress. This is your first post. Edit or delete it, then start writing!

With most themes, including Astra theme, the name links to the author page, which shows all articles written by that author. Incidentally, that author page also has its own RSS feed.

Try it!

Add **feed** to the end of the author page URL and you should see the XML code of the RSS feed.

The next few options are for contact information.

Contact Info

Email *(required)*   jack_spratt@harlun.co.uk

Website

The only one that is required here is the email address and we have talked earlier about how important that is. If you want to fill out the website field, you can, but this is more useful if you have multiple authors on your site, each with their own personal website.

Next in the profile is your **Biographical Info**.

About Yourself

Biographical Info   Andy Williams is an online instructor teaching a variety of courses on webmaster related skills. Check out his site at ezseonews.com.

Share a little biographical information to fill out your profile. This may be shown publicly.

Profile Picture

You can change your profile picture on Gravatar.

I recommend you fill in a short biography as some themes (including Astra) will show this on the author page:

Andy

Andy Williams is an online instructor teaching a variety of courses on webmaster related skills. Check out his site at ezseonews.com.

Hello world!

1 Comment / Uncategorized / By Andy

Welcome to WordPress. This is your first post. Edit or delete it, then start writing!

The Profile picture can be added by setting up a Gravatar. This is just an image linked to your email address. The photo will then appear on your author page, and on any websites where you leave a comment using that email address.

At the bottom of the User Profile screen, you have an **Account Management** section.

Account Management

New Password   Generate Password

Sessions   Log Out Everywhere Else

Did you lose your phone or leave your account logged in at a public computer? You can log out everywhere else, and stay logged in here.

Update Profile

The first button allows you to generate a secure password to use with your account. If you are using a weak password, click the **Generate Password** button, copy the new password for your records, and then click the Update Profile link at the bottom.

The other tool in this section is a security measure that allows you to log out of WordPress everywhere except "here". Imagine your laptop was stolen and you hadn't logged out of your Dashboard. The **Log Out Everywhere Else** button has your back. Click that and the only place you will remain logged in is the computer you were at when you clicked the button.

Let's set that up now.

Gravatars

A Gravatar is simply a photograph or image that you can connect to your email address.

Sites that use Gravatar information, like WordPress, will show that image whenever possible if you contribute something.

For example, your photo will show on your author page. It will also show on any WordPress site where you leave a comment (assuming you use that photo-linked email address when leaving the comment). Some themes can even show your photo after each post along with your author's bio.

Here is the box that appears after every post of mine on the ezseonews.com website:

About Andy Williams

Dr. Andy Williams is a Science teacher by training, but has now been working online for over a decade, specializing in search engine optimization and affiliate marketing. He publishes his free weekly Internet Marketing newsletter with tips, advice, tutorials, and more. You can subscribe to his free daily paper called the Google Daily and follow him on Facebook orTwitter. You can also follow me on Google +

View all posts by Andy Williams →

OK, let's set up the Gravatar.

Go over to Gravatar.com and find the button or link to sign up.

You'll be asked to fill in your email address, pick a username, and choose a password. Note that this username and password is nothing to do with your WordPress site. This is a unique username and password for use on the Gravatar site.

Follow the on-screen instructions.

Gravatar.com will send an email to your email address. You need to open it and click the confirmation link to activate your new Gravatar account.

On clicking that link, you'll be taken back to a confirmation page telling you that your WordPress.com account has been activated. You can then start using Gravatar by clicking the Sign in button.

When you log in you will then be taken to a screen that allows you to assign a photo to your email address:

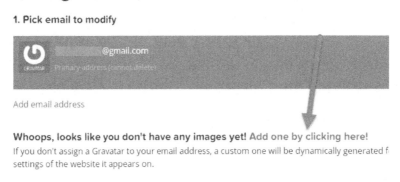

Just click the link and you'll be able to choose an image from a number of different places, including upload, from a URL, or from a webcam.

Once you've selected your image, you'll get an option to crop it.

You now need to rate your image (remember, we mentioned Gravatar ratings earlier when setting up WordPress):

Just click the appropriate button.

That's it. Your Gravatar should now be attached to your site's email address. Whenever you leave comments on a WordPress site, use that email address and your image will show up along with your comment (assuming they haven't turned Avatars off).

Tasks to Complete

1. Go and claim your Gravatar.
2. Log in to your WordPress site and complete your user profile.
3. Find a WordPress site in your niche and leave a relevant comment making sure to use the same email address you registered for a Gravatar. Watch as your image appears next to your comment.

Tools

The next main menu is called Tools, and it has six options:

The **Available Tools** screen simply tells you how to convert your categories to tags, or vice versa.

Tools

Categories and Tags Converter

If you want to convert your categories to tags (or vice versa), use the Categories and Tags Converter available from the Import screen.

Clicking on the link will take you to a screen that lists a number of different tools, including the Categories and Tags Converter. If you want to use this or any other plugin on the import screen, I suggest you read the **Details** for the plugin by clicking the link under the plugin title.

The next option in the **Tools** menu is **Import**. This takes you to the same screen we've just seen. The import plugin is the last one on the list. Install it, and you'll then be able to "Run Importer" to import posts that you have previously exported from another WordPress site.

RSS
Install Now | Details
Import posts from an RSS feed.

Tumblr
Install Now | Details
Import posts & media from Tumblr using their API.

WordPress
Run Importer
Import posts, pages, comments, custom fields, categories, and tags from a Wor export file.

If the importer you need is not listed, search the plugin directory to see if an importer is available.

We probably should have covered the **Export** tool before the import tool. The Export feature allows you to export content from your site in a format that can be easily imported into another WordPress site. I have used these features when I wanted to merge two or more websites into one larger website. Let's see the process.

To export content, click the **Export** menu:

Export

When you click the button below WordPress will crea

This format, which we call WordPress eXtended RSS c

Once you've saved the download file, you can use the

Choose what to export

⦿ All content

This will contain all of your posts, pages, comments, cu

◯ Posts

◯ Pages

◯ Media

Download Export File

You can choose to export all the site content, posts, pages, or media files.

If you select posts, you will be given more options including categories to export, export by author, date range or status (published, scheduled, draft, etc.).

Once you have made your selection, click the export button to download the export file to your computer.

To import the content into another website, install the relevant WordPress plugin on the Import screen:

RSS   Import posts from an RSS feed.
Install Now   Details

Tumblr   Import posts & media from Tumblr using their API.
Install Now   Details

WordPress   Import posts, pages, comments, custom fields, categories, a
Install Now   Details   export file.

Click the **Install Now** link.

Once installed, the link under the plugin changes to **Run Importer.**

Click the **Run Importer** link and you'll see the following screen:

Choose the file and click **Upload file and import.**

You will then have the chance to assign the content you are importing to a new or existing user:

If you have images or other media in the exported content, check that box **Download and import file attachments** to make sure everything comes across.

When you click the **Submit** button, the content will be imported.

The next menu is for **Site Health.**

Site Health

◯ Good

Status   Info
_____

Site Health Status

The site health check shows critical information about your WordPress configuration and items that require your attention.

3 recommended improvements

You should remove inactive themes	Security	∨
One or more recommended modules are missing	Performance	∨
Your site does not use HTTPS	Security	∨

Passed tests ∨

At the top, under the heading, you'll get an overall rating. Mine says **Good**, as I suspect does yours.

There are then two tabs. Once for status and one for info.

The status health screen gives you important information about your WordPress installation. As you can see from the screenshot above, mine has three suggestions. The first one is to remove inactive themes, which we mentioned earlier. If you do remove all inactive themes, you'll get this message:

| Have a default theme available | Security | ∧ |

Themes add your site's look and feel. It's important to keep them up to date, to stay consistent with your brand and keep your site secure.

Your site has 1 installed theme, and it is up to date.

Your site does not have any default theme. Default themes are used by WordPress automatically if anything is wrong with your normal theme.

Manage your themes

It is, therefore, a good idea to install one of the WordPress default themes in case of emergencies. Do that now. Go and search for the Twenty Twenty theme and install it if you removed it earlier. You'll then find that recommendation disappears from the list.

Do your best to fix any security issues that arise here. Performance issues are more general recommendations. E.g. you probably have a note that some PHP modules are missing. Don't worry about these. You can talk to your web host about the missing modules if you want, but I have never seen one that was vital to add.

If you need to contact WordPress or your host about issues you are having, click onto the **info** tab, and copy the site info to the clipboard.

Site Health

◯ Good

Status   Info

Site Health Info

This page can show you every detail about the configuration of your WordPress website. For any improvements that could be made, see the Site Health Status page.

If you want to export a handy list of all the information on this page, you can use the button below to copy it to the clipboard. You can then paste it in a text file and save it to your device, or paste it in an email exchange with a support engineer or theme/plugin developer for example.

[Copy site info to clipboard] ⬅ ②

WordPress   ⌄

Directories and Sizes   ⌄

You can then paste the text into a support email to send.

The next Tools submenu is **Export Personal Data**. This can be used to export a zip file containing the data that has been collected about a user on your site. This will help you comply with privacy laws if a user requests a copy of the data you have about them.

The **Erase Personal Data** will allow you to delete a user's personal data upon verified request. This deletion is permanent and cannot be reversed. If a user ever requests their personal data is deleted, this is the tool for you.

Appearance Menu

The **Appearance** menu contains these items:

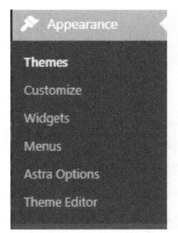

This menu, as the name suggests, gives you access to settings that control the appearance of your site. The **Astra Options** menu was obviously added by that theme.

Clicking on the Appearance menu opens the themes page.

At the top of the themes screen, you have the option to **Add New** theme, which will search the WordPress theme repository for approved (and therefore generally safe) themes that you can install and use on your site. We've already seen how this works.

NOTE: You will often hear people referring to WordPress themes as templates. While the two things are not totally the same thing, people often use the words interchangeably to mean the same.

If you have more than one theme installed, you'll see a thumbnail of each one. There will also be a search box at the top to help you search your installed themes.

Since we recommend removing inactive themes (with the exception of one default WordPress theme), you probably won't need the search feature on this page.

Your active theme is shown in the first position, with a **Customize** button bottom right. Clicking this button is the same as clicking the **Customize** item in the **Appearance** menu. It will take you to a live editor allowing you to make some design changes to the appearance of your site.

Customize Live Editor

Open the live editor by clicking on the customize button or the Customize item in the Appearance menu.

On the left is a menu that gives you access to site settings.

Most of these settings can also be found buried in the dashboard's **Settings** menu. The advantage of editing them here is you get to see a live preview when you do make changes. The live preview is the large window on the right.

The settings you see in the left menu will depend on the theme you have installed. If you installed Astra as I suggested, your menu will look like the one above.

Near the top, you can see the name of the active theme and a button which allows you to change themes if you want. Clicking that change button will open a screen that shows you the currently installed themes as well as giving you the options to look for themes on wordpress.org.

Under the active theme section of the menu are the main configuration options for your active theme.

Global	>
Header	>
Breadcrumb	>
Blog	>
Sidebar	>
Footer	>

Reminder: If you are not using the Astra theme, you won't have the same settings options. Also, if you have upgraded to the Astra Pro version, you will have more options available.

I'll go through these Astra settings quickly, but do have a look around yourself and experiment. You can't break anything 😊

Global – These are options that affect the entire site, and include options for:

- Typography – to change the base font family used for headings and content.
- Colors – to change the base colors to be used for text, links, background color, etc.
- Container – specifying how wide the content container is for your site. That is the width to be taken up with content. You also have options for the layout of that content like boxed and full-width.
- Buttons – allowing you to choose the color of buttons on your site, and the borders around the button.

Header – These settings refer to the very top part of your web page which we call the header. Options with the Astra theme include:

- Site Identity – where you can specify a logo, site icon (favicon), site title and tagline.
- Primary Header – where you can specify the layout of the header section.
- Primary Menu – Where you can disable the menu in the header, add a search box or other items, as well as configure how the menu appears on mobile devices.
- Transparent Header – which makes the header transparent and gives you some color options.

Breadcrumb – which allows you to define breadcrumb navigation on your site. This is the typical navigation you get at the top of a web page like this:

Home » Juicer Reviews » What is the Best Juicer for Beginners?

What Is The Best Juicer For Beginners?

Blog – Gives you options for configuring the post structure for posts on your website. This includes simple on/off switches to toggle the display of those items on or off.

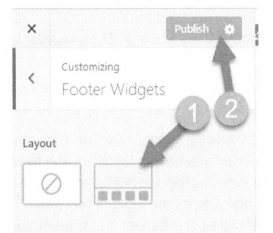

Sidebar – Allows you to choose what kind of sidebar you want to be used by default on posts, pages, and archive pages. Right, left, or none. You can even specify the width of the sidebar.

Footer – Controls what is displayed in the footer area of your site. If you want to include widgets in the footer areas, you will need to activate them here:

The **Footer Bar** section of these settings allows you to customize the copyright information shown in the footer.

Under the footer menu, we have 4 more menu items:

Menus   >

Widgets   >

Homepage Settings   >

Additional CSS   >

Menus – allows you to configure the menu system on your site, and add them to predefined locations (these are defined by the theme you are using).

Widgets – allows you to configure the widgets on your site. Note that you will only see enabled widget areas in this section. On my site that is:

Main Sidebar	>
Footer Bar Section 2	>

This is different from the Widgets screen accessed from the Appearance menu, which shows all widget areas whether they have been enabled or not:

Main Sidebar	▲	Footer Widget Area 1	▼
Meta	▼	Footer Widget Area 2	▼
Header	▼	Footer Widget Area 3	▼
Footer Bar Section 1	▼	Footer Widget Area 4	▼
Footer Bar Section 2	▼		

Homepage Settings – This allows you to specify what you want on your homepage. Latest posts or a static page.

Additional CSS – If you want to tweak the design on your site using CSS, this option allows you to add custom CSS without having to edit CSS files. The advantage of adding custom CSS in this way is that it won't be overwritten if your theme updates itself. CSS is beyond the scope of this book.

Widgets

The widgets menu will take you to the widgets screen. Click on that now.

Widgets are basically plugins that allow you to easily add visual and interactive components to your site without needing any technical knowledge.

If you want to add a list of recent posts, you can do it easily by using a widget. Perhaps you want to add a poll to your site? Well, that can be done with widgets too.

When a designer creates a WordPress theme, their initial drawing will probably have "widgetized" blocks drawn onto it, so that they can visualize which areas will accept widgets. Maybe it will look something like this (with the shaded areas able to accept the widgets):

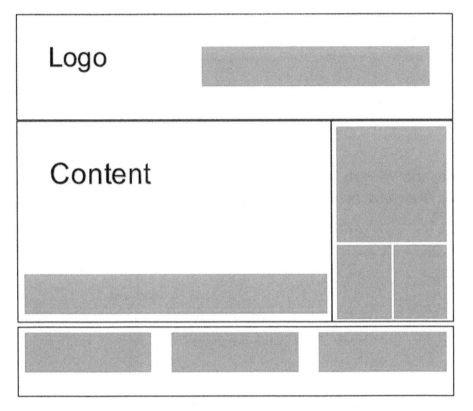

The usual areas that accept widgets are the header, sidebars, and footer. Sometimes you can also add widgets after post content.

With the Astra theme, we have already seen there are a number of areas that can accept widgets.

Main Sidebar ▲	Footer Widget Area 1 ▼
Meta ▼	Footer Widget Area 2 ▼
Header ▼	Footer Widget Area 3 ▼
Footer Bar Section 1 ▼	Footer Widget Area 4 ▼
Footer Bar Section 2 ▼	

Remember though that with Astra, most of these are disabled by default.

Each of these collapsible boxes represents the areas on the site that can accept widgets.

If you remember, when we were clearing out the pre-installed widgets, I left that one so I could have a quick-link to log in to my website. You can see it in that screenshot. It's the **Meta** widget in the sidebar section. That widget creates this feature in the sidebar on my website:

If I wanted to remove those links from my site, I'd simply delete that widget.

Have a play around with the widgets. Drag and drop them from the list on the left, into the sidebar on the right. Then go and look at your site to see what that widget added.

Hopefully, you can see the potential of widgets.

Basic HTML

When adding a text widget, one thing that will come in handy is some simple HTML code. For example, if you want to add some text with a link to another page, you'd just look up the HTML below for creating a hyperlink and insert it into your text widget accordingly.

A Hyperlink

<a href="URL">LINK TEXT</a>

Just replace URL with the web address of the page you want to link to, and LINK TEXT with the word or phrase you want to be linked.

Example:

If you are interested, you can read my review of the <a href="http://blenderreview.com/waring">waring blender</a> for more details.

If I entered that into a sidebar text widget, it would look like this on my site:

I added a title to the text widget (Example link). You can see the phrase "Waring blender" is a link to the URL I specified in the HTML.

An Image

To insert an image, here is the HTML:

```
<img src="URL" width="XX" height="YY" />
```

Replace URL with the URL of the image (upload it via the media library and grab the URL there), XX is the width in pixels and YY is the height in pixels. If your image is the correct size (which it should be to keep image load times to a minimum), then you can leave out the height and width parameters and the code just becomes:

```
<img src="URL" />
```

For example, using an image from my media library, I grabbed the URL for the image and inserted it into a text widget. This is what it looks like:

IMAGE INSERTED

That's a 32-year-old me!

A Numbered List

The HTML for a numbered list is a little more complicated.

```
<ol>
  <li>item one</li>
  <li>item two</li>
  <li>item three</li>
```

```
</ol>
```

You simply replace item one, item two, item three and so on with whatever you want displayed. You can add as many items as you need. Just repeat the <li>**item**</li> code once for each item you want to add.

For example, here is some code that shows a numbered list of my top three tablet recommendations.

```
<ol>
  <li>Asus 301</li>
  <li>Asus 201</li>
  <li>Apple iPad</li>
</ol>
```

.. and this is what it looks like in a sidebar text widget.

AN EXAMPLE LIST

1. Asus 301
2. Asus 201
3. Apple iPad

NOTE: The text you add for an item CAN be a hyperlink. Just construct it from the HTML I showed you above.

A Bullet List

A bulleted list is almost the same code as the numbered list with one modification.

Instead of the code opening with <ol> and closing with </ol>, a bullet list opens with <ul> and closes with </ul>. The "ol" stands for ordered list (ordered by number), whereas the "ul" stands for unordered list.

```
<ul>
  <li>item one</li>
  <li>item two</li>
  <li>item three</li>
</ul>
```

Here is my widget now:

A BULLET LIST

- item one
- item two
- item three

That should give you enough HTML to get you started with text widgets.

Menus

The **Menus** screen inside the **Appearance** menu takes you to a screen that will allow you to build menu systems for your site, and specify where they go in your site design. Since we don't have any content on the site yet, we cannot create a menu. Therefore, we'll look at menus later on.

Astra Options

This item will take you to the Astra theme options. The links in the top part of the table send you back to the relevant section of the Customize screen we saw earlier:

Links to Customizer Settings:

Upload Logo	Set Colors
A Customize Fonts	Layout Options
Header Options	Blog Layouts
Footer Settings	Sidebar Options

There is also a section for Pro users of Astra. If you need that extra power offered by the Pro version, check out the Astra sales page here:

https://ezseonews.com/astra

At the bottom of the Astra settings page is a list of free plugins you can use with your copy of Astra. These all work with the free version of Astra, and you can enable them directly on the settings screen. If you want to activate any of these, please do. You won't break anything and you can easily deactivate them once you are done.

The Theme Editor Menu

The bottom item in the **Appearance** menu is the **Theme Editor**. This allows you to edit the theme's PHP files. This is an advanced topic requiring programming skills, so we won't be covering it here.

Tasks to Complete

1. Make sure you have Astra installed.
2. Go to the Customize screen and go through all of the option screens to familiarize yourself with them.
1. Go and explore the widget area. Add some widgets to your site and then view the site in your browser to see what they do and how they format the information.
2. Add in a text widget and experiment with the HTML code I gave you in this chapter. Try adding a text widget to the top of the sidebar with a photograph of yourself and a brief bio.

Plugins

In this section, I want to explain what plugins are, where you can get them, and how to install them. I'll also walk you through the installation and configuration of a few important plugins.

In the Dashboard sidebar, you'll see the **Plugins** menu:

The "1" in a red circle means there is one plugin to update. See earlier in the book on how to update plugins, themes, and WordPress itself.

The menu has three options:

Installed Plugins – To view the current list of installed plugins.

Add New – To add a new plugin. You can also add a new plugin from the **Installed Plugin** screen.

Editor – This is a text editor that allows you to modify the code of the plugins. We won't be looking at this advanced topic.

Click on the installed plugins menu to go to the plugins screen. Here is mine (yours may look different):

Plugins [Add New]

All (4) | Active (2) | Inactive (2) | Update Available (1)

Bulk Actions ▼ [Apply]

Search installed plugins...

4 items

At the top of this screenshot is this:

All (4) | Active (2) | Inactive (2) | Update Available (1)

All, **Active**, **Inactive** and **Update Available** are all groups of plugins. The number of plugins in each group is represented by the number in brackets.

I have a total of 4 plugins installed on this site, 2 are active, 2 inactive, and 1 needs updating.

You may see something slightly different. For example, if you have deactivated a plugin that was once active, you might also see another group called **Recently Active**. You may also have a group called **Drop-ins** depending on the plugins you have installed. These are special types of plugins that alter core WordPress functionality.

To activate a plugin is easy. Just click the **Activate** link underneath the name of the plugin.

The menu at the top will change to reflect the newly activated plugin.

All (4) | Active (3) | Inactive (1) | Update Available (1)

Bulk Actions ▼   Apply

Deactivating is just as easy. The **Deactivate** link is present for all active plugins.

Plugin	Description
Akismet Anti-Spam Settings Deactivate	Used by millions, Akismet is quite possibly the best way in your blog from spam. It keeps your site protected even wi started, just go to your Akismet Settings page to set up yo Version 4.0.1	By Automattic	View details

We can view just the active plugins, or just the inactive plugins, by clicking those links at the top:

NOTE: It is not a good idea to keep inactive plugins installed. If you do not need a plugin, deactivate and delete it.

For security reasons, whenever you see the **Update Available** group, go in and update the plugin(s). Click the update available link to see which plugins have updates pending.

All (4) | Active (3) | Inactive (1) | **Update Available** (1)   Search installed plugins...

Bulk Actions ▼   Apply

Plugin	Description
Akismet Anti-Spam Settings Deactivate	Used by millions, Akismet is quite possibly the best way in the world to protect your blo from spam. It keeps your site protected even while you sleep. To get started, just go to Akismet Settings page to set up your API key. Version 4.0.1	By Automattic	View details
	⟳ There is a new version of Akismet Anti-Spam available. View version 4.0.2 details or update now.
Plugin	Description

Once updated, the **Update Available** link at the top will disappear.

As you saw earlier, you can also handle all updates by using the Dashboard's **Updates** menu.

I don't want to use Akismet or Hello Dolly (these were pre-installed with WordPress), so let's delete them now.

NOTE: Akismet is a good anti-spam plugin but it went commercial a while back, meaning it's no longer free for commercial websites. If your site is non-profit, feel free to activate Akismet.

Deleting Plugins

To delete a plugin, it needs to be inactive. If you have an active plugin you want to delete, first deactivate it.

To delete a plugin, click the **Delete** link under the plugin name (the delete link only appears on inactive plugins):

You will be asked to confirm the deletion, so click OK. The plugin and all its files will be removed from your server.

If you have more than one plugin to delete, there is a quicker way to remove multiple plugins in one go:

Just check the box next to each plugin you want to delete, then, in the **Bulk Actions** drop-down box at the bottom, select **Delete**.

Click the Apply button to carry out the deletion. You will get a confirmation screen like the one we saw a moment ago, asking you to confirm that you really do want to delete all selected plugins.

NOTE: The bulk action drop-down box also allows you to activate, deactivate, and update multiple plugins in one go.

Plugin-Injected Menu Items

Some plugins may add their own menu items, like this one:

This upgrade link takes you to a website to buy an upgraded version of the plugin. Don't let that confuse you with the updating of plugins we saw earlier. Since plugins (and themes) are created by third-party programmers, this type of extra menu item is quite common.

Installing Important Plugins

Before we look at the plugins, I need to let you know that plugins are updated frequently, and their appearance may change a little. However, these changes are usually minor cosmetic changes, so if you don't see exactly what I am showing you in these screenshots, look around. The options will be there somewhere.

Let's go ahead and install a few very important plugins, then configure them.

UpdraftPlus

Backing up anything on a computer should be a priority. While good web hosts do keep backups for you, if your site gets infected with any kind of malicious code and you don't find out about it for a while, all their backups could be infected.

I always recommend you have your own backup plan, and fortunately, there is a great plugin that can help.

Click the **Add New** item in the **Plugins** menu.

Search for **Updraft**.

Find, install, and activate, this plugin:

You'll have a new **UpdraftPlus Backups** section in the settings menu. Click on it to access the settings of this plugin.

You can take manual backups on the **Backup/Restore** tab:

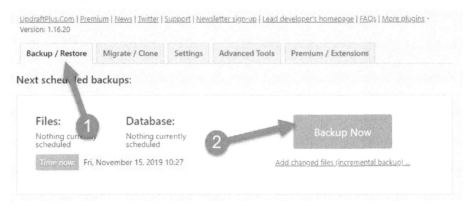

More powerful still is the ability to schedule automatic backups of your site. To do that, click on the **Settings** tab.

Choose a frequency and the number of backups to retain.

Now scroll down and click **Save Changes** at the bottom.

You will notice that on this screen, you also have the option of using remote storage for your backups. If you have a Dropbox account, that is a great place to send backups. They'll be off your server, and safe if you ever need them.   You can also get backups emailed to you, though full backups can be very large.

I won't go into details on setting this up, just follow the instructions that are included with the plugin.

Contact Form 7

It's important that site visitors can contact you, so let's install the best-known contact form plugin. It's called Contact Form 7.

Install and activate the plugin.

This will add a new menu called Contact in the sidebar of the Dashboard.

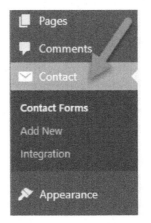

If you click on **Contact Forms**, you can see that the plugin created one for you.

We will use this one, as it is a perfectly good contact form. You just need to copy the **Shortcode**. That's easy enough. Just click the shortcode and it will highlight the entire code ready for copying.

Create a new page by clicking on **Add New** in the **Pages** menu.

Add a title for the page, e.g. Contact Form, Contact, or Contact Us.

Now click your mouse into the block that says "Start writing…."

Contact

⊕   Start writing or type / to choose a block

You are actually clicking into a "paragraph" block. Ideally you would want to add a shortcode block (more on blocks when we look at the Gutenberg editor) to hold this shortcode, however, WordPress will recognize the shortcode in a paragraph block, so simply paste in the code.

Contact

[contact-form-7 id="28" title="Contact form 1"]

Publish the page using the publish button at the top. You'll need to also click the second publish button that appears.

You can now visit the page by clicking on the **View Page** link:

Published ✕

Contact is now live.

What's next?

Page address

http://wordpress-for-beginners-2020.l...

View Page   Copy Link

When the page opens, you will see the contact form.

WP-Insert for "Legal Pages"

The legal pages are the important documents you need on your site from a legal point of view. We've already seen the Privacy Policy earlier, but others include Terms of Service, Disclaimer, etc.

Ideally, you would want a lawyer to draw these up for you because no plugin is going to be 100% complete, or take your personal needs into account. There are also web services out there where you can buy packs of legal documents you can update and use.

So, with that said, be aware that while I will show you a plugin to add these to your site, it is only to get you up and running quickly. I'd still recommend you get proper legal documents drawn up.

There are a few plugins out there that can create quick legal pages. The one I suggest you look at is called WP-Insert.

Wp-Insert

The Ultimate Adsense /
Ad-Management Plugin
for Wordpress

By Namith Jawahar

Install Now

More Details

★ ★ ★ ★ ☆ (133)

20,000+ Active Installations

Last Updated: 4 months ago

Untested with your version of
WordPress

Install and activate it.

You'll find a new menu in the sidebar navigation labeled **Wp Insert**. Click on it to open up the settings.

Now, this plugin does a lot more than just generate legal pages. It's also a full-blown ad manager, which is useful if you want to put adverts or AdSense on your site.

For legal pages, we need to scroll down to the "Legal Pages" section:

Legal Pages

Legal Page Templates to kick start your Legal Notices.

Privacy Policy

Terms and Conditions

Disclaimer

Copyright Notice

You can see that this plugin can create a Privacy Policy (which you should have created earlier, so probably don't need), Terms and Conditions, Disclaimer and Copyright Notice. You create all of these pages in the same way, so I'll just go through one with you.

Click on the Terms and Conditions link.

A dialogue box pops up with the information you need to read.

Notice that the plugin recommends you get proper legal advice for this type of document. That echoes the advice I gave you earlier.

Also, note the three tabs on the left. Disclaimer, Content and Assign Page(s).

Click on the **Content** tab. You will see the default content of the Terms and Conditions page. You can edit this if you want.

Now click on the **Assign Page(s)** tab.

Click the **Click to Generate** button.

The plugin will create a page for the document. Once done, you can see it selected in the **Assign a Page** box:

To confirm this is correct, click the **Update** button.

If you click on the **Pages** link in the sidebar navigation to view all of your pages, you will now find the Terms and Conditions page.

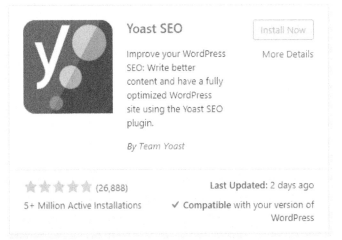

Click on the **View** link to open the page in your web browser.

Repeat for other legal documents you want to create.

Yoast SEO

Go to **Add New** plugin and search for **Yoast SEO**.

Install and activate the plugin.

This plugin installs a new menu in the sidebar called **SEO**.

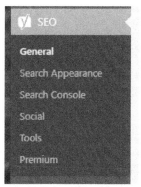

Click on the **General** link in the SEO menu.

Across the top, you'll see some tabs – Dashboard, Features, and Webmaster Tools.

Click on the **Features** tab to see a list of features you can enable and disable. Currently, all of them are enabled by default. I am not going to go through what each of these does, but I will tell you that I disable SEO Analysis and Readability analysis because I don't find them very useful. While SEO analysis is a nice idea, it does focus on a single keyword optimization (in the free Yoast SEO plugin) which is something I stay away from. Google hates content that is highly optimized around a single keyword, so paying too much attention to this feature can only get you into trouble in my humble opinion.

One option that I do want to highlight is the XML sitemap feature. Click on the "?" icon next to this feature to open up a little more information and a link to your own sitemap.

XML sitemaps ❓

Enable the XML sitemaps that Yoast SEO generates. See the XML sitemap. Read why XML Sitemaps are important for your site.

On   Off

If you click on the link to **See the XML Sitemap**, it should open in a new window:

XML Sitemap

Generated by YoastSEO, this is an XML Sitemap, meant for consumption by search engines

You can find more information about XML sitemaps on sitemaps.org

This XML Sitemap Index file contains 3 sitemaps.

Sitemap	Last Modified
http://localhost/wordpress/post-sitemap.xml	2018-10-01 14:44 +01:00
http://localhost/wordpress/page-sitemap.xml	2018-10-02 09:56 +01:00
http://localhost/wordpress/category-sitemap.xml	2018-10-01 14:44 +01:00

Only content that has been published will show on the sitemap, so what you see will depend on the stage of development your site is at. If you have published content but do not see the sitemap, then make sure:

1. WordPress is installed on an online web host and not on your own computer (an advanced technique some developers use).
2. You have published posts or pages.
3. Yoast SEO settings have been saved to ensure the feature is enabled.
4. If it still doesn't show anything, go to the **Permalinks** section (inside the **Settings** menu of the sidebar navigation) and just scroll to the bottom to save the permalink structure.

The sitemap should now appear.

Now click back on the **Dashboard** tab at the top of the General Yoast SEO settings.

You'll see a box that says **First-time SEO configuration**. In the box is a link to the configuration wizard. Click the link.

You'll be taken through a multi-step procedure to configure the plugin.

I won't go through the wizard here as it changes a lot and by the time you read this, it may already look different. Just follow along and answer the questions as you go.

If you are unsure of any answers, just accept the default setting.

The last screen of the wizard is promotional, so don't be lured into buying something you don't need 😊.

By the time you have finished the wizard, the plugin will have made some necessary changes to your WordPress install, even adding in something called "structured data" for your posts and pages. Structured data is beyond the scope of this book, but essentially it gives Google extra information that can be used to create rich snippets in the search results. If you want to learn more about structured data, please see my course on the subject. A link to all of my courses can be found at the end of this book.

OK, click on **Search Appearance** in the SEO menu.

Across the top you can see several tabs:

Notice also the help button underneath. The built-in help with this plugin is excellent, so do go in and watch the video to learn more about the many features this plugin can offer you.

These tabs setup how the different types of content are displayed on your site, and in the search results. Have a look through the settings, but leave everything with the default values.

Finally, click on the **Social** link in the SEO menu. This is where you can go in and add/edit the social media links you set up with the wizard.

OK, for now, we are done with the Yoast SEO plugin.

WordPress Security

I would recommend you check out a free plugin called All in One WP Security.

All In One WP Security & Firewall

A comprehensive, user-friendly, all in one WordPress security and firewall plugin for your site.

By Tips and Tricks HQ, Peter Petreski, Ruhul, Ivy

Install Now

More Details

☆ ☆ ☆ ☆ ☆ (914)

800,000+ Active Installations

Last Updated: 3 weeks ago

✓ Compatible with your version of WordPress

It is a great way to secure your WordPress website from hackers. I'll warn you that the plugin is quite complicated and can lock you out of the Dashboard if you set it up too aggressively. I, therefore, won't be covering it in this book. I simply don't want readers to face problems and then have no one to ask for help.

If you want to see a video tutorial I created for setting up this plugin, you can watch it here:

https://ezseonews.com/secureit

If you want a more comprehensive look at WordPress Security, including a more detailed set of tutorials for this plugin, I have a course called "WordPress Security – How to Stop Hackers". Check out the link at the end of this book.

Akismet Anti-Spam

WordPress may install Akismet by default. It is an excellent anti-spam plugin that is free for non-commercial sites. However, if you have a commercial site, the plugin does require you pay for a commercial license.

When you activate the plugin, you'll see a banner across the top of your dashboard:

Plugins Add New

Set up your Akismet account   Almost done - configure Akismet and say goodbye to sp

Plugin activated.

All (8) | Active (6) | Inactive (2)

Bulk Actions ▼ Apply

	Plugin	Description
☐	**Akismet Anti-Spam** Settings · Deactivate	Used by millions, Akismet is quite possibly the best your site protected even while you sleep. To get sta key. Version 4.0.8	By Automattic	View details

Click the setup button.

A screen opens that has a button to **Get your API key**. Click it and you'll be taken to the Akismet plugin page.

Click the button to Activate Akismet. You'll be taken to a pricing table to select your plan. Follow the instructions to get your API key.

Once you have your key, paste it into the API Key box and click on the **Connect** button.

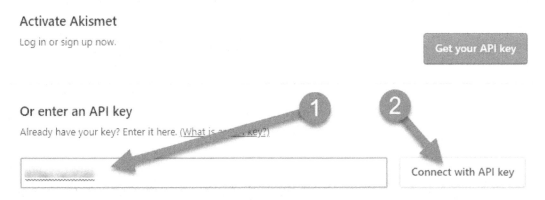

You will see a few options, but essentially your site is now protected from spam by Akismet.

Tasks to Complete

1. Delete any pre-installed plugins.
2. Install Updraft Plus and set it up.
3. Create a contact form using Contact Form 7.
4. Install WP-Insert and create the "legal" pages.
5. Install Yoast SEO and run through the wizard to set it up.
6. Check your sitemap is working.
7. Consider installing and configuring the All-In-One Security plugin.
8. Activate Akismet if you want to use it, and get your API key.

Comments

I mentioned earlier that a lot of people turn comments off because they can't be bothered with comment moderation. The way I see it, comments are the life and soul of a website and help to keep visitors engaged with you and your content. You need to offer visitors this chance to connect with you. Therefore, you really should keep comments turned on.

We have already configured the "discussion" settings to blacklist comments with known spam content (using the blacklist you found by searching on Google), and that will cut down on comment spam considerably. However, there are dedicated anti-spam plugins available as well.

If you are running a non-commercial website, I recommend you use Akismet. It is probably the best anti-spam plugin available. It is for non-commercial use only though, and commercial sites need to pay for it.

I am reluctant to recommend a free comment spam plugin because most of the ones I have tried did not work effectively. The All-In-One Security plugin I recommended earlier in the book does include some great anti-spam features, so do investigate those. You will find them in the **Spam Prevention** menu within the main menu of the plugin.

I personally use a plugin called WP-SpamShield. It is excellent, but it is not free. Search Google if you want to look at that one.

Moderating Comments

When people comment, their comments won't go live until you approve them. This is how we set the site up earlier. If you had comments set on auto-approve, you'd most likely find so many spam comments on your site that you'd be pulling your hair out. Manual approval is the only way to go, and it does not have to take a long time.

Let's see how easy it is to moderate comments.

If you click on **Comments** in the sidebar, you are taken to the comments section.

Across the top is a menu with All, Mine, Pending, Approved, Spam & Trash:

Lower down you can see a comment I added to the site. When I added the comment, I used an email address linked to a Gravatar. That's why my photo is there. When you leave a comment on a WordPress site, your photo will show up too if you use a Gravatar-linked email address.

If you hover your mouse over a comment in the list, a menu appears underneath that comment, which you can click to Approve, Reply, Quick Edit, Edit, Spam & Trash.

If the comment is OK, click the Approve link. If the comment is clearly not spam, but you don't want to approve it, then click on **Bin**. If the comment is spam, click the spam link.

NOTE: Remember the **WP All-In-One Security** plugin? It has a nice feature that will automatically block comments from the IP addresses of comments in the spam folder. You'll find that by using this feature, you can improve spam recognition, and make your job of moderation easier.

You can also edit comments if you want to remove something (like a link) or correct a spelling error from an otherwise good comment.

I recommend you don't reply to comments until you approve them. My typical workflow is this:

1. Moderate comments.
2. Go to the Approved comments by clicking the Approved link at the top.
3. Reply to comments that need a reply.
4. Go to the **Bin** and empty it.

In the screenshot above, you will see a (0) next to the spam link. That means there are no spam comments. However, if you have any, click on the spam link to see what the spam folder contains.

You can see the comment and author for each comment in the list. If you decide that a comment is not spam, mouseover it and click **Not Spam** from the menu. The comment will be sent to the **Pending** pile and await moderation.

You also have the option to **Delete Permanently**. To delete all spam in the spam folder, you can simply click the **Empty Spam** button at the bottom. When you do delete spam, it is permanently removed.

The **Bin** holds all comments that were sent to the "trash". Like the Spam folder, you can retrieve comments that are in the Bin (if you need to) using the mouseover menu.

Finally, we have the **Approved** list. These are all comments on your site that have been approved.

Click the link in the menu at the top to view them.

All comments in the Approved list have a mouseover menu as well, allowing you to **Reply** to the comment if you want to. You can, of course, change your mind about an "approved comment", and send it to spam or trash if you want to, or even **Unapprove** it if you want to think about it.

What Kinds of Comments Should you Send to Spam/Bin?

You will get a lot of comments that say things like "nice blog", or "Great job". I suggest you trash all comments like this because they are spam comments. Their only purpose is to try and get a backlink from your site to theirs, through flattery.

I recommend you only approve comments that:

1. Add something to the main article, either with more information, opinions or constructive information. That means never approving a comment that could have been written without that person ever reading your post. Comments MUST add something to your content. If they don't I suggest you send them to the Trash.

2. Never approve a comment where the person has used a keyword phrase for their name. You'll see people using things like "best Viagra online", or "buy XYZ online" as their name. No matter how good the comment is, trash it. What many spammers do is copy a paragraph from a good webpage on another website, and use that as their comment. The comment looks great, but the name gives away the fact that the comment is spam.

3. I would suggest you never approve trackbacks or pingbacks. Most will not be real anyway.

With comments, be vigilant and don't allow poor comments onto your site as they will reflect badly on both you and your website.

Here are three spammy comments left on one of my websites. All three would go straight to spam without hesitation:

These comments are totally irrelevant to the content they are commenting on. You'll get a lot of comments like this. Spammers seem to think that a bit of flattery is all that is required to get a comment approved.

Also, check out the names of the "people" leaving each comment.

Tasks to Complete

1. Install an anti-spam plugin if you want to use one, or look into the anti-spam features of the All-In-One Security plugin and enable those.

2. Whenever there are comments on your site, moderate them. Spam or Trash any comments that are not "adding to the conversation".

Media Library

Media includes things like images and videos that you want to use in posts, as well as other downloads you want to offer your visitors, e.g. PDF files.

The media library is a convenient storage area for all such items.

You can go and have a look at your Media Library by clicking on **Library** in the **Media** menu. All items are shown as a thumbnail. Clicking on a thumbnail will open the **Attachment Details** screen, which shows you the media item, URL, Title, etc. You even have some basic editing features if you need to crop, scale or rotate an image.

Uploading stuff to your media library is really very easy.

You will usually add media directly from the **Add Post** screen when typing a piece of content. However, if for example, you have a lot of images that you want to upload at any one time, it is often quicker to do it directly in the Media library.

How to Upload New Media

Click on **Add New** in the **Media** menu, or, on the **Media Library** page, click the **Add New** button at the top.

Uploading media is as simple as dragging and dropping into the dashed box:

Upload New Media

Drop files to upload

or

Select Files

You are using the multi-file uploader. Problems? Try the browser uploader instead.

Maximum upload file size: 300 MB.

(You can also click the **Select Files** button and select them directly from your hard disk.)

Note that there will be an upload limit that is stated under the dashed box. This tells you the maximum size of uploads on your server. Mine is 300MB, yours may be different. If you need something bigger, you need to talk with your web host about it as they need to change settings within your hosting package.

To drag and drop something, open the file manager on your computer. Select the file(s) you want to upload and click and hold the left mouse button on the selected items. Now move your mouse, dragging the items to the dashed box in the Media Library screen. You can then release the mouse button, dropping those files into the Media Library.

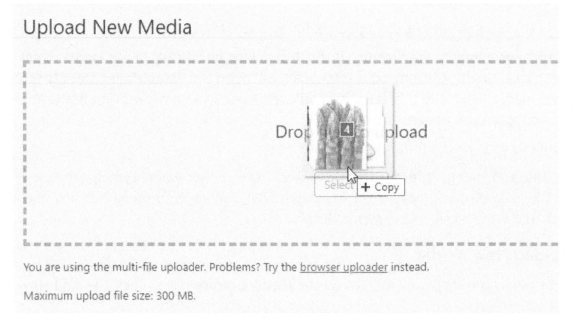

NOTE: You may see something a little different when you drag your images over the box. In the screenshot above, I entered the "Upload Media" screen by clicking on the **Add New** link in the Media menu. However, if you clicked on the **Library** menu item first and then clicked the **Add New** button, things are a little different. Try it and see.

When you drop images in the dashed rectangle, they are uploaded to the library. When the upload is complete, you'll be shown a list of uploaded images:

You are using the multi-file uploader. Problems? Try the browser uploader instead.

Maximum upload file size: 300 MB.

avocado		Edit
bananas		Edit
blueberries-xs		Edit
asparagus heads		Edit

Clicking the Edit link to the right of this thumbnail to open the **Edit Media** screen. This screen allows you to add a caption, ALT text, and description, for the "attachment" page that is created for your image.

To access the actual attachment page created, click the permalink at the top of this screen:

Have a look at the URL of that attachment page. The URL will use the filename of the image to construct the web page's filename.

Chances are you won't actually use this page on your site unless you run some kind of image/photo site. However, know that it's there.

Click on **Library** in the **Media** menu.

You should see your uploaded images:

What you see depends on which view you have selected. See those two icons top left? Click on each one to see what they do.

In the screenshot above, you can see that the images I uploaded are not "attached". An unattached image means it is not being used on any post or page. We will look at how to add an image (or video) to a post later in this book. But for now, just try uploading a few images to get the hang of things.

NOTE: The media library is there to provide a central location for all of the media files you want to use on your site. This is not limited to images. You can upload other file formats like PDF, MP4, etc.

However, there are some file formats that WordPress will not let you upload for security reasons. PHP files are one example. If you want to upload a file to offer as a download on your site, but it is not accepted for upload, then zip it up and upload the zipped file instead.

At the top of the media library screen, you'll see some filtering options:

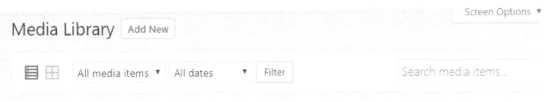

The two drop-down boxes allow you to view only a specific type of media, e.g. images, or only those media items that were uploaded in a particular month.

We've already looked at the first two buttons that change the view of your uploaded media. Select that first button to show the table view.

When viewing your media library in the "list view", each item has the now-familiar mouse-over menu which allows you to **Edit**, **Delete Permanently**, or **View,** that media item.

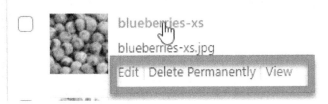

There is a column showing you the date the item was added to your library.

Note that columns in the media library are sortable by clicking the title of the column.

Mouse over a column header to see an "ascending/descending" arrow and click to re-order.

If there are columns you don't use and don't want to see, you can hide them by using the screen options. Remember those?

Columns

☑ Author   ☑ Uploaded to   ☑ Comments   ☑ Date

Pagination

Number of items per page: 20

Apply

Just unclick whichever items you don't want to see. You can even specify how many media items you see per page in your library.

If you have a lot of media in your library, there is a handy search feature:

In the screenshot above, I entered blue and hit the return key. The results returned the one media item including the word "blue". The search feature will look for your search text in both the title of the media and its description. If the word appears in either, it is shown in the search results.

To cancel the search filter, click on the "X" in the search box:

.. and press enter to refresh the results.

The media library also gives you **Bulk Actions** (something that can be applied to multiple items in one go).

Next to each media item is a checkbox. If you want to delete several media items, you can check each one, and then select **Delete Permanently** from the **Bulk Actions** drop-down box. Click **Apply** to delete the checked items.

That's it for the Media Library for now. We will come back to this when we look at how to add content to your site.

Tasks to Complete

1. Go and explore the media library. Practice uploading a photo, video, or sound file, and grabbing the URL.

2. Try using the search feature to find a specific piece of media in your library.

Pages v posts

When you want to add written content to your site, you have two options. You can either create a **Page** or a **Post**. In terms of adding/editing, these two are very similar, but they are actually quite different in terms of function.

This may sound confusing to people who are new to WordPress (or maybe even new to website building). After all, isn't a post on your site a page? Doesn't a page on your site contain a post?

For some reason, WordPress creators decided to name these two types of content "posts" and "pages" and it does cause confusion. However, you do need to understand the basic differences between them when it comes to building your site. The information I'll give you later will make it easy for you to decide which to use, so don't start panicking.

Since WordPress was originally designed as a blogging platform (i.e. to help build websites that were constantly updated with posts about whatever was going on in that blogger's life), posts were designed for these regular, chronological updates.

WordPress **posts** are *date-dependent and chronological,* and this separates them from **pages** which are date-independent and not really related to any other piece of content on the site.

Posts were originally designed to be ordered by date. A post you created yesterday should logically appear lower down the page than a post you make today. Newer posts are inserted at the top of the page, and older posts are pushed off the bottom. If you think back to the WordPress reading settings, we saw that the default homepage of a WordPress site shows posts in this manner.

A typical blog will be structured this way. Let's look at an example.

Suppose you were keeping a blog about your weight loss program. On day one you weighed in at 210lb, so you write about that and what you have done for the day to help with your diet. Each day you write a new entry as a kind of personal journey on your weight loss progress.

When someone comes to your site, they see the daily posts in chronological order. This means visitors to your 'blog' can follow your story logically and see how your diet is working out for you.

This type of chronology is not possible with pages (well it is, but it takes a lot of effort plus plugins to achieve, so why bother?). Pages do not have any defined order, though they can have a hierarchy of parent and child pages.

OK, so date-dependency is one important difference between WordPress posts and pages. What else?

Well, posts can be categorized, pages cannot (at least not without plugins).

Suppose you were creating a site about exercise equipment. You might have a series of reviews on different treadmills, another set of reviews on exercise bikes, and so on.

Using posts allows us to categorize our content into relevant groups. If I had 10 reviews of various weight loss programs, I could create a category on my site called weight loss programs and add all

10 reviews to this category by writing them as posts.

Putting related content into the same category makes sense from a human visitor point of view, but also from the point of view of a search engine. If someone were on your site reading a review of the Hollywood Diet, it would be easy to use features of WordPress posts to highlight other reviews in the same category. This can be done with posts, but it is a much more manual process if you tried doing the same thing with pages.

Posts can also be tagged with related words and phrases.

Tags are an additional way to group and categorize your content. We'll discuss tags later, but for now, just realize that they can be used to further categorize your content to help your visitors and the search engines make sense of your project.

It is possible to create tags for pages as well, but once again, only with plugins. As a rule, we try not to use plugins unless they are essential, as they can slow down the loading time of a website, and possibly add security vulnerabilities if they are not well maintained by their creators.

Another great feature of posts is that they can have **Excerpts**. These are short descriptions of the article that can be used by themes and plugins to create a Meta description tag or a description of the article in a list of related articles. For example, below is a related posts section (created using a plugin), on one of my websites. It shows excerpts being used for the post descriptions:

Related Posts:

- Omega-3 Fatty Acids Omega-3 fatty acids are vital to health and are essential in your diet. This article looks at the health benefits, deficiency etc.
- The Ratio of Omega-6 to omega-3 Essential Fatty Acids Redressing the omega-6 to omega-3 ratio is easy. You simply cut out foods high in omega-6s and take fish oil supplements with omega-3 fats.
- Too Much Too Little Omega-3 – Finding the Balance Fish oil from supplements can help to redress the imbalance of omega-6 to omega-3. Too little omega-3 can have negative health consequences.

Another important feature of posts is that they appear in your site's RSS feed. Remember, we talked about how important RSS feeds are, earlier in the book. RSS feeds highlight the most recent posts, but pages are not included.

When to Use Posts and When to Use Pages

OK, this is the million-dollar question that I get asked a lot!

This will depend on the type of website you want to build. For a lot of company websites, using pages for most of the content makes sense, like this:

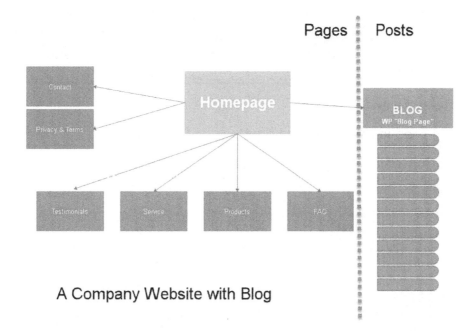

Pages | Posts

A Company Website with Blog

Everything to the left of the dotted line is a Page. Everything to the right is a Post.

In this model, the company site uses WordPress "pages" for all of the main important content that they want to convey to visitors. That includes homepage, contact, legal pages, testimonials, services, products, and FAQ. These pieces of content are all isolated and unrelated to one another. And that is where a page comes in useful.

The company site also has a blog, and in this model, the blog is built with posts. From the point of view of this company, what features of posts make them ideal for the blog?

The fact that posts are chronological, maybe? That means the company can post product updates, with the latest announcements at the top!

The main type of website I personally build uses a different model. It is a model that particularly suites niche sites, eCommerce, etc. It's a model that relies on the fact that a piece of content does not live on an island, it is related to other pieces of content, which can be grouped and categorized.

This model offers great SEO benefits as well as organizing content in a logical manner to help both visitors and search engines.

Before I tell you the model, let me first distinguish between two types of content that you may have on your site.

The first type of content is your "call to action" stuff. It's the content you want your visitors to see. The content you want ranking high on Google. We'll call this type of content, **Niche Content**. This will include articles, reviews, videos, infographics, etc. that **you create for your site and your targeted audience**.

The second type of content is the stuff that you need to have on the site, but from a financial point of view, you don't really care whether visitors find it. This type of content does not fit into logical groups as we saw with posts. Typical examples would be a Privacy page and Terms of Service. I'd also add the "contact" and "about us" pages to this grouping. I call this type of content my "legal pages".

Do you understand the difference?

Here is the basic rule I used in this website model.

Use Posts for "Niche Content", and Pages for "Legal Pages".

Here is a diagram of the model:

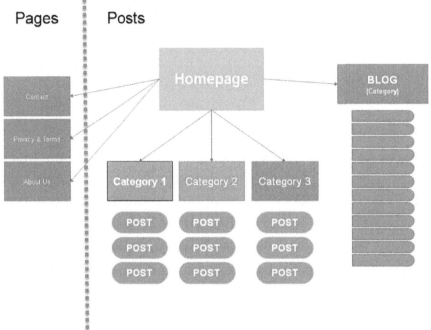

A typical Niche / eCommerce Site

On the left of the dotted line, you can see the pages. On the right (with the exception of the homepage which uses a static page), they are all posts.

It's a simple enough rule, and it will make perfect sense when we start adding pages and posts to the website. Before we can do that though, we need to look at post categories and tags.

Categories and tags are only relevant to posts. Pages don't use them. Therefore, if you decide you want to create a site that mainly uses pages, you can skim over the next chapter.

Tasks to Complete

1. Go over this section until the differences between pages and posts are clear in your mind.
2. Can you make a list of any legal pages you may require on your site?

Categories & Tags

Before we can start adding posts to our site, we need to think about the way the site will be structured and how the posts will be organized within the site.

We have already touched on categories and tags earlier in the book and have set up the SEO settings for these taxonomies. Let's have a closer look at categories and tags so that you can fully understand them and add a few to your site.

Both categories and tags are ways to categorize your posts.

All posts MUST be assigned to a category, but tags are optional. Categories are, therefore, more important than tags.

Think of categories as the main way to organize your posts. Think of tags as an additional organizational tool, that can be called upon if needed.

Let's look at an example.

Let's consider a website about vacuum cleaners. What would your main categories?

If you had a bunch of vacuum cleaner reviews, how would you want them organized?

Possibly more importantly, how would your website visitors expect them to be organized?

Here are some ideas for categories:

- Dyson
- Handheld
- Dyson Ball
- Eureka
- Bagless
- Cordless
- Hoover
- Upright
- Canister
- Miele
- HEPA filter

All of these could be categories, but then you might get to the situation where one post might fit into several categories. While WordPress encourages this, I recommend you put each post into ONE category only (for SEO purposes). Forcing yourself to think of one category per post can actually help you find the best categories for your site.

Of those ideas listed above, which ones would make the most sense if a vacuum could only be in one category?

How about "bagless"?

Nope. A vacuum could be bagless, upright and a Dyson.

The obvious categories from that list would be the ones where a vacuum could only fit into one - the brand names. My categories would therefore be:

- Dyson
- Eureka
- Hoover
- Miele

A Dyson DC25 vacuum cleaner review could only go into one category – the Dyson category.

So, what about the other terms:

- Handheld
- Dyson Ball
- Bagless
- Cordless
- Upright
- Canister
- HEPA filter

A vacuum could be cordless, bagless, and contain a HEPA filter! That's a clear indication that these features are not suited as categories, however, they are perfect as tags!

For example, my review of the Dyson DC25 vacuum would be in the category Dyson but could be tagged with ball, HEPA, bagless & upright.

The beauty of using tags is that for every tag you use, WordPress will create a page just for that tag. The tag page will list ALL posts that have been assigned that tag. In the example above, WordPress would create FOUR tag pages. One for "ball", one for "HEPA", one for "Bagless" and one for "Upright".

The "HEPA" tag page will list all vacuums on the site that have been tagged with HEPA – it helps visitors find more HEPA vacuums if that is what they are interested in.

The "Bagless" tag page would list all vacuums on the site that were bagless (and therefore tagged with that term). A visitor to my site looking for a bagless vacuum could use the tag page to quickly see all available bagless vacuums that had been reviewed to date.

Tags help search engines too. They provide additional information about an article, helping search engines understand what the content is about.

There is no doubt that tags are powerful. However, with that power comes some responsibility. If you abuse tags, your site will become spammy.

I have seen sites where posts have been tagged with 10, 20, 50, and even several hundred tags. Don't believe me? See this screenshot showing the tags for a post on one website I came across:

You don't need to be able to read the words in that screenshot to get the point. I've had to reduce the size of the screenshot to get all the tags into view. There are over 160 tags for that single post. I happen to know that Google penalized that site.

Every tag on that list will have its own tag page.

The biggest problem for that site is that many of the tags used on that post are not used on any other posts. That means there are 100+ tag pages with just a single post listed as using that tag.

To think about this in another way, if a post lists 160 tags, and this is the only post on the website, then the site will contain over 160 pages. It'll contain one post, 160 tag pages which are all nearly identical (as they all just list the same post), and a few other pages that WordPress creates for us, which will actually be almost identical to the 160 tag pages.

The way the webmaster used tags in this example is clearly spam, and search engines hate spam. Please, use tags responsibly!

Let's look at one more example.

Think of a recipe website about puddings, desserts, cakes and so on.

You might have main categories like:

- Ice cream
- Cakes
- Muffins
- Mousse
- Cookies

These are the obvious categories since a dessert will only be able to fit into one of the categories. To further classify the recipes on the site, we'd use tags that would add a little more detail about each post.

What type of tags would you use?

Stuck for ideas?

Tags usually choose themselves as you add more content to a website. For example, you might find that a lot of recipes use chocolate, or walnuts, or vanilla, or frosting (you get the idea). These would make perfect tags because a visitor with a hankering for chocolate could visit the chocolate tag page and see a list of all ice cream, cakes, muffins, mousse and cookies that include chocolate.

Do you see how the tags help with additional layers of categorization? The tag pages become useful pages for visitors.

This is the mindset you are looking to develop as you utilize tags for your own website.

A Few Guidelines for Using Tags

1. Keep a list of tags you use on your site and make sure you spell them correctly when you reuse them. Remember, if you misspell a tag, another tag page will be created for the misspelled version.
2. Don't create tags that will only apply to one post. Remember, tags are there to help classify your content into groups. Most tags will be used several times on a site, and its use will increase as you add more content. I'd recommend that you only use a tag if it will be used on 3 or more posts.
3. Only pick a small number of relevant tags per post. I'd recommend somewhere between 3 – 6 tags per post, but if some need more, then that's fine. If some need less that's OK too. This is just a general rule of thumb.
4. NEVER use a tag that is also a category.

Setting Up Categories & Tags in Your Dashboard

Categories and tags are properties of posts, so you'll find the menus to work with them under the **Posts** menu in the sidebar.

Categories and tags can either be set up before you start writing content, or added as you are composing it. The most common method is to set up the main categories before you begin, but add tags while you are writing your post.

I recommend that you create a description for all tags and categories, and to do that, you will need to go into **Categories** editor and **Tags** editor using the Posts menu.

OK, let's go and set up a category first. Click on the **Categories** menu:

On the right, you will see a list of current categories.

Bulk Actions ▼	Apply				1 item
☐ Name		Description	Slug	Count	
Uncategorized Edit Quick Edit View		—	uncategorized	1	
☐ Name		Description	Slug	Count	
Bulk Actions ▼	Apply				1 item

There is only one category – Uncategorized. WordPress set this up for you during the WordPress installation. Since it is currently set as the default category for posts, it cannot be deleted. We could create another category and then make it the default for posts. We could then delete the Uncategorized category. However, we can just change the name of the uncategorized category so it is useful for the site.

If you mouseover the category, you'll see a menu appear under the title (see the screenshot above).

Quick Edit will allow you to change the category name AND the category slug. The slug is just the text that is used in the URL to represent the category of the post. Remember we set up Permalinks earlier to look like this:

/%category%/%postname%/

The %category% variable is replaced by the category slug and the %postname% variable will be replaced by the post name.

WordPress will automatically create the slug when you save your category. To create the category slug, WordPress uses the same text as the category name (converted to lowercase), with any spaces replaced by a dash.

Therefore, a category name of **juicer reviews** would have a default slug of **juicer-reviews**, but you can specify your own slug if you prefer not to use the WordPress default.

OK, let's edit the Uncategorized category.

Click on the **Edit** link under the **Uncategorized** name.

Edit Category

Name	Uncategorized ←
	The name is how it appears on your site.
Slug	uncategorized ←
	The "slug" is the URL-friendly version of the name. It is usually all lowercase and contains only letters, numbers, and hyphens.

Enter a new name for your default category, and leave the **slug** box empty, like this:

Edit Category

Name

Krill Oil

The name is how it appears on your site.

Slug

The "slug" is the URL-friendly version of the name. It is usually all lowercase and contains only letters, numbers, and hyphens.

Parent Category

None ▼

Categories, unlike tags, can have a hierarchy. You might have a Jazz category, and under that have children categories for Bebop and Big Band. Totally optional.

Description

Krill Oil is a rich source of Omega-3 and Astaxanthin, an antioxidant many times more powerful than vitamin C.

The description is not prominent by default; however, some themes may show it.

Update

Enter a description for your category.

When you are done, scroll to the bottom of the page and click the **Update** button.

Now click the **Back to Categories** link at the top of the page:

Edit Category

Category updated.

← Back to Categories

WordPress will use the name of the category as the basis for the slug. That will become the text that is used in the URLs of all posts in the category.

Name	Description	⋮	✎	Slug
Krill Oil	Krill Oil is a rich source of Omega-3 and Astaxanthin, an antioxidant many times more powerful thank vitamin.	●	●	krill-oil
Name	Description	⋮	✎	Slug

The description will be used as the Meta Description of the category page.

When we were editing the category, you might have seen an option to specify a parent category. I didn't mention it at the time, as there is no "parent" for my default category, but what is a parent category?

Parent Categories & Hierarchy

Categories can be hierarchical. In other words, you can have categories within categories.

An example might be a website on car maintenance. I might have a category called Toyota, but then want sub-categories called Yaris, Auris, Prius, Land Cruiser, etc. etc.

Therefore, the parent category would be Toyota. When I create the Yaris, Auris, Prius, Land Cruiser categories, I'd select Toyota as the parent.

Add New Category

Name

Yaris

The name is how it appears on your site.

Slug

The "slug" is the URL-friendly version of the name. It is usually all lowercase and contains only letters, numbers, and hyphens.

Parent

Toyota

Categories, unlike tags, can have a hierarchy. You might have a Jazz category, and under that have children categories for Bebop and Big Band. Totally optional.

In the list of categories, you can spot parent/child relationships because the parent category is listed first, with the child categories indented below:

Name	Description	🔢	✎	Slug
Toyota	—	●	●	toyota
— Land Cruiser	—	●	●	land-cruiser
— Prius	—	●	●	prius
— Auris	—	●	●	auris
— Yaris	—	●	●	yaris

Parent/Child categories are very useful for tidying up the navigation menus on your site.

Imagine if you had 10 different cars from each of 5 manufacturers. That would be 50 categories for your site. That is a lot of categories to display in a menu!

By using parent-child categories, you can just have the 5 main manufacturers in your menu, with the model of the cars only visible when selecting its parent.

Adding a New Category

Adding a new category is easy.

Click the **Categories** menu from inside the **Posts** menu.

Fill in the name, slug (if you want to), and a description. Then select a parent if applicable. Click the **Add New Category** button and your new category is ready for use.

OK, let's look at the Yoast SEO settings for categories.

Click on **Categories** in the **Posts** menu.

Move your mouse over a category and click the **edit** link.

Scroll to the bottom of the screen, and you'll see the Yoast SEO settings.

These settings are added by the Yoast SEO plugin that we set up earlier.

This is what you'll see:

You can see what the category page will look like if listed on Google. That is your search engine listing, more or less. You can see that there is no description for that category page, so to edit aspects of this listing, click on the **Edit Snippet** button. You'll then be able to edit the SEO title, Slug and Meta Description for this category page.

The social tab allows you to specify title, description, and images that are used when your category page is shared on Facebook or Twitter.

Yoast SEO

Back on the SEO tab, you can see an Advanced section. Click on that:

There is an option there to specify whether or not this category page can be indexed by Google.

If you made any changes, be sure to click the **Update** button to save them.

Adding Tags

Adding Tags is very similar to adding categories except tags cannot have a parent-child relationship with each other.

For every tag you enter, add a description to explain what that tag is being used for. That description will then be used for the Meta Description of the tag page; this is how we set it up within the SEO plugin, remember?

Like the categories, the **Add Tag** screen has just a few options – Title, Slug, and Description. You only need to fill in the Title and Description because WordPress will handle the slug for us. However, if you go in and edit an existing tag, you will see extra Yoast SEO settings for the tag. These are identical settings to the Category edit screen but do go in and have a look.

While I expect you will add tags directly on the **Add Post** screen as you write your content, I do highly recommend you come back to this section every time you use a new tag, just to fill in a description for those tags you create. When you make a new tag on the **Add Post** screen, you don't have the option of adding the description there and then, but it is important to add one nonetheless.

Tasks to Complete

1. Set up a few categories for your site.
2. Think about possible tags and keep a list on a notepad.
3. Make sure to add descriptions to every tag and category that you add.

Writing Posts

In this section of the book, I want to look at publishing content on your site. Version 5.0 of WordPress changed things dramatically. The old WYSIWYG editor (now called the Classic editor) was replaced by a page builder system called Gutenberg.

The two systems are VERY different.

The good news is that with the introduction of Gutenberg, WordPress created a "Classic Editor" plugin that can be installed, so you have a choice. You can use the new Gutenberg page builder, or install the plugin and use the classic "WYSIWYG" editor. The choice is yours.

I will cover both editors here, so you know the main differences, then the choice is yours. If you want to install the Classic editor, install and activate this plugin:

Once installed, click on the **Settings** link:

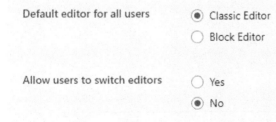

The plugin has added its settings to the Writing Settings page, which makes sense considering this plugin helps you write content. There are two main settings you can change:

The first one defines which editor you want to use by default. The Block editor option refers to Gutenberg. The second option is whether you want users to be able to switch back and forth between the Classic Editor and Gutenberg.

Choosing the Classic Editor or Gutenberg

If you want to use Gutenberg, then don't install the Classic Editor plugin. All posts and pages will then be created in the Gutenberg editor.

If you want to use the classic editor, install and activate the plugin. All "add post" and "add page" links will then default to the Classic editor.

Let's look at how you can add content, first using the Classic editor, then using Gutenberg. If you installed the Classic Editor plugin, then follow along. If you are intent on only using Gutenberg, then ignore this section.

Adding a Post With the "Classic" WYSIWYG Editor

The toolbar of the editor (the place where you add your content), looks like this:

If you only see one line of buttons on your toolbar, click the **Toggle Toolbar** button on the right. That will expand the toolbar.

You'll see on the top right there are two tabs – **Visual** & **Text**.

The Visual tab is where you can write your content using WYSIWYG features. On this tab, you'll see text and media formatted as it will appear on the website once published. This is the tab you will want to use for most of the work you do when adding new, or editing existing content, on your site.

The other tab – Text - shows the raw code that is responsible for the layout and content of the page. Unless you specifically need to insert some code or script into your content, stick with the Visual tab.

The two rows of buttons allow you to format your content visually. If you have used any type of Word Processor before, then this should be intuitive.

I won't go through the functions of all these buttons. If you need help understanding what a button does, move your mouse over it to get a popup help tooltip.

Adding content to your site is as easy as typing it into the large box under the toolbar. Just use it like you would any word processor.

Write your content. Select some text and click a formatting button to apply the format. Make it bold, or change its color, make it a header, or any of the other features offered in the toolbar.

To create a headline, enter the headline and press the return button on your keyboard to make sure it is on its own line. Now click somewhere in the headline and select the headline from the drop-down box in the toolbar.

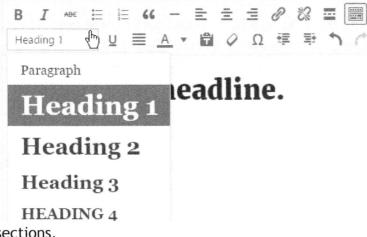

NOTE: WordPress themes typically show the title of your post as an H1 header at the top of the page. This is the biggest header available and is equivalent to the **Heading1** in the drop-down selector. You should not use more than one H1 header on a web page, so avoid using the **Heading 1** as you write your content. Use **Heading 2** for main sections within your article, and **Heading 3** for sub-headers inside **Heading 2** sections.

OK, it's now time to go ahead and write the post, for your website.

As you write your article, you may want to insert an image or some other form of media. We looked at the Media library earlier in the book, but let's go through the process of adding an image to an article.

Adding Images

The process is straightforward.

Position your cursor in the article where you want to add the image. Don't worry too much about getting it in the right place because you can always re-position it later if you need to.

Click the **Add Media** button located above the WYSIWYG editor, to the left, and you'll see the popup screen that we've seen previously:

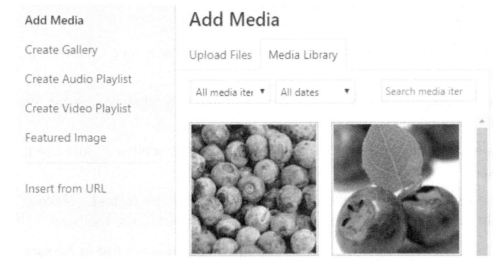

From this screen, you can select an image from the media library, or click the **Upload Files** tab to upload a new image to the media library.

Let's add an image from our Media Library.

Click the **Media Library** tab if it is not already selected and click on the image you want to use in the post.

A checkmark appears in the top right corner of the image, and the "attachment" details are displayed on the right side. These image details can be edited if you want to.

At the bottom of the right sidebar is an **Insert into post** button. Before you click that, we should consider a few of the sidebar options.

One important option is the **Alt Text**. This text is read to the visually impaired visitors on your site and helps them understand what images are being shown. Therefore, add a short descriptive ALT text. For my example, **blueberries** is sufficient.

At the bottom of the right-hand column (you may need to scroll down) are some **Attachment Display Settings**. Currently, my image is set to "none" for alignment.

I want to align the image to the left so can select that from the drop-down box.   When an image is aligned left (or right) in WordPress, the post text wraps around it. If you select **None** or **Center** for alignment, the text won't wrap.

The next option you have is to link your image to something. The default setting is **None**, meaning we insert an image that is not clickable by the visitor because it is not linked to anything. Most of the time, I'll use none. However, if you want the image to open up when clicked (e.g. in a lightbox), then select **Media file**.

You can also link an image to an **Attachment page** (which we saw earlier), or a **Custom URL**.

The **Custom URL** option is really useful. This allows you to navigate to a URL when a user clicks an image. For example, if your image is a "Buy Now" button, you'd want the image linked to the purchase page.

The last of the display settings is **Size**. You'll be able to choose from **Full size** and **thumbnail**. The dimensions are included with each file size, so choose the one that is closest to the size you want the image to appear on your page.

I want my image to be full-sized (as I had resized the image to the correct size before I uploaded it to the media library), so I'd select **Full Size**.

Once you have made your selection, click the **Insert into post** button at the bottom.

Here is that image inserted into my post at the position of my cursor:

tempor incididunt ut labore et dolore magna aliqua. Leo duis ut diam quam nulla porttitor. Justo donec enim diam vulputate ut pharetra.

Nulla aliquet porttitor lacus luctus accumsan. Ut enim blandit volutpat maecenas volutpat blandit aliquam etiam erat. Est ante in nibh mauris cursus mattis molestie. Quam viverra orci sagittis eu. In est ante in nibh mauris cursus mattis molestie. Pellentesque pulvinar pellentesque habitant morbi. Aliquet nec ullamcorper sit amet. Non sodales neque sodales ut. Mi proin sed libero enim. At auctor urna nunc id cursus metus aliquam eleifend mi. Odio eu feugiat pretium nibh ipsum consequat. Viverra mauris in

If you have the position wrong, you can simply click the image to select it, and drag the image to a different location.

If you find that the image isn't inserted as you intended (e.g. you forgot to align it), click on the image. A toolbar appears above the image and a bounding box around it:

The bounding box includes a small square in each corner. You can use this to resize the image. Drag one of the corners to make the image bigger or smaller.

The first 4 buttons in the toolbar allow you to re-align the image.

The last button in the toolbar will delete the image.

The toolbar edit button looks like a pencil. You can use this to open the **Image Details** screen to make a number of changes:

Image Details

Alternative Text | Tasty Asparagus

Describe the purpose of the image. Leave empty if the image is purely decorative.

Caption |

DISPLAY SETTINGS

Align | Left | Center | Right | None

Size | Custom Size ∨

Width | Height
283 | × | 369
Image size in pixels

Link To | None ∨

Edit Original | Replace

You'll also see a link to **Advanced Options** at the bottom. Click that to expand the advanced options:

ADVANCED OPTIONS ▲

Image Title Attribute |

Image CSS Class |

☐ Open link in a new tab

Link Rel |

Link CSS Class |

The advanced option that is most useful to us is the **Open link in a new tab** option. When someone clicks the image, whatever it is linked to opens in a new browser tab.

Once you have made your edits on this screen, click the **Update** button and the changes will be updated in your post.

You can insert videos from your Media library in the same way.

OK, finish your first post.

Something to try: We added an image that was already in the Media Library. Go ahead and add an image from your hard disk. After clicking the Add Media button, you'll need to go to the Upload tab to proceed. Try it and see if you can successfully add an image this way.

Once you've done that, try adding an image to a post by dragging and dropping the image from your computer directly into the WYSIWYG editor window.

It's all very intuitive.

There are a few things we need to do before we publish a post, so let's go through the complete sequence from start, to publish:

1. Add a post title.
2. Write & format your post using the visual text editor (WYSIWYG).
3. Select a post format if available. You can ignore this option for most posts you add.
4. Select a category.
5. Add some tags if you want to. Tags can always be added later, so don't feel under any pressure to add them now. Of course, you can also decide you don't want to use tags on your site. That is fine too.
6. Add an excerpt.
7. Select a date/time if you want to schedule the post for the future.
8. Publish/Schedule the post.

OK, so far we have completed down to step 2.

Post Formats

Not all WordPress themes use "Post Formats". The Twenty Sixteen theme that we are using does and you can see them on the right of your screen:

Since most, if not all your posts, should use the default (Standard), we won't go into details in this book about other formats. Most people just won't use them and not all themes support them.

If you are interested in post formats, experiment with them. Select one and update your post. Then view your post to see how it looks. You can also read more about Post Formats on the WordPress websites:

http://codex.WordPress.org/Post_Formats

Post Category

The next step in our publishing sequence is to choose a category. Choose just one category for each post.

If you forget to check a category box, WordPress will automatically use your default category.

You can add a new category "on the fly" from within the **Add post** screen, but if you do, remember to go in and write a description for the new category so it can be used as the meta description of that category page (remember the Yoast SEO plugin we set up earlier is expecting a description of categories and tags).

Post Tags

If you want to use tags for the post, you can type them directly into the tags box, even if they don't already exist. When you are finished typing the tags, click the **Add** button to the right of the tags box.

As you add and use more tags, you can click on the link **Choose from the most used tags** and a box will appear with some of the tags you've used before. You can just click the tags that apply and they'll be added to the tag list of your post.

If you add new tags when entering a post, remember to go into the Tags settings to write a short description for each one. Yes, it takes time. However, this will be used as the Meta description of the tag page.

Post Excerpt

You should add a post excerpt to all posts. If you don't see an excerpt entry box on your screen, check the **Screen Options** to make sure **Excerpt** is checked.

NOTE: Screen options are not available if you are you using the Gutenberg editor, but that doesn't matter as excerpts are enabled by default in Gutenberg.

Once checked, the **Excerpt** box magically appears on your edit post screen.

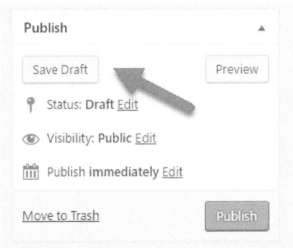

The excerpt should be a short description of the post you are writing. Its purpose is to encourage visitors to click through and read the article (e.g. From the search engine). This excerpt will be used as the Meta description tag of the post, as well as the description of the post in the "related posts" section, which is displayed at the end of each article you publish (see the YARPP plugin later).

Enter a three to five sentence excerpt that encourages the click.

Publishing the Post

The next step in the process is deciding when you want the post to go live on your site. Let's look at the **Publish** section of the screen.

The first option you have is to save the post as a draft.

Once saved as a draft, you can go back at any time to make changes or publish the article. Draft posts are not shown on your site. To be visible on your website, you need to publish the post.

If you want it up there immediately, then click the Publish button. If like me, you are writing several posts in a batch, it is a good idea to spread the posting of the content out a little bit. Luckily, WordPress allows us to schedule posts in the future.

The default is to publish **immediately**. However, there is an **Edit** link you can click to open a scheduling calendar:

Enter the date and time you want to publish the post and then click the OK button.

The publish button now changes to **Schedule**.

Click the **Schedule** button to schedule the post.

That's it. You've just published or scheduled your first WordPress post using the Classic editor.

If you now click on the **All Posts** in the sidebar menu, you will see your new post listed. If you mouse over, you'll see that you are given the option of editing the post in the Classic Editor (which created the post), or the Block Editor (Gutenberg).

Title	Author	Categories	Tags
Classic Editor in Action — Classic Edit	Andy	Krill Oil	—
Edit (Block Editor) Edit (Classic Editor) Quick Edit Trash View			
Hello world! — Block Editor	Andy	Krill Oil	—

The option for editing this post with Gutenberg was added when you selected the option to allow switching editors.

Adding a Post with the Gutenberg Editor

Gutenberg is the default editor in WordPress. I am therefore going to stick with it from now on. To that end, I am going to uninstall the Classic editor plugin. If you want to stick with Gutenberg, I recommend you do too.

If you've ever used a WordPress "page builder" like Elementor, then Gutenberg will seem a lot more familiar to you. Like other page builders, Gutenberg uses a system of blocks to help you build your content. On adding a new post or page, you'll be greeted with the Gutenberg editor:

There is a simple prompt: **Add title**.

Click into that box, and you can type the title of your post.

Under the title is your first "paragraph" block (for adding text), kindly added by Gutenberg:

Move your mouse over this block and you'll see some icons appear on the right. The images you see may be different from the ones in my screenshot. The icons in my screenshot are to change this paragraph block to an "image block", "heading block" and "gallery block".

If you just want to add some text below the heading, click into the block and start typing. If you want to add an image, click the **Add Image** icon. If you want to add some other type of block, click the + symbol in the circle. This opens up the block browser:

The search box at the top makes it easy to find the block you want, but that will become more useful as you learn what is available. This menu is one way to add new blocks to your post. We've already seen those icon buttons as another way to choose a block. There is also the **Add Block** button in the top toolbar on the page:

This again opens up the block editor.

With Gutenberg, you build your web pages using blocks.

In its simplest form, a post could be simply a title and a **paragraph** block, like this:

The Gutenberg Editor

Gutenberg is the new block editor built into WordPress 5.0. It is a big change from the traditional classic editor, but fortunately you can still access that editor using the Classic Editor plugin.

Note that there is only one paragraph per block. If you are writing a block of text, and press the Enter key to start a new paragraph, Gutenberg will automatically create a new paragraph block for the second paragraph. In the following screenshot, I pressed the Enter key after the final word of the first paragraph:

The Gutenberg Editor

Paragraph

Gutenberg is the new block editor built into WordPress 5.0. It is a big change from the traditional classic editor, but fortunately you can still access that editor using the Classic Editor plugin.

A lot of people choose to install the Classic Editor plugin because they have used it for many years and do not want to switch.

Can you see that Gutenberg automatically created a new paragraph block? Go on and try it for yourself.

This auto-addition of new paragraph blocks makes writing long pieces of content very easy because you do not need to manually create paragraph blocks as you type.

If you tend to write your content in an external editor and then paste it into WordPress, you'll find that Gutenberg automatically splits the text into multiple paragraph blocks for you!

The advantage of using one block per paragraph is that each paragraph can then be formatted independently of the others.

Paragraph Block Properties

All blocks have their own properties. Since we've added a paragraph block, let's check out the properties because you can do some interesting stuff. Click into a paragraph block. On the right-hand side, you should see the **Block** tab has been selected:

Document   Block   ✕

¶   Paragraph
     Start with the building block of all
     narrative.

Text Settings   ∧

Font Size
Normal ∨

Drop Cap
Toggle to show a large initial letter.

Color Settings   ∨

Advanced   ∨

The **Block** tab shows you the settings for that block only (as opposed to the **Document** tab which has settings affecting the entire document). You can select the size of the text for that paragraph by choosing an option from the drop-down box:

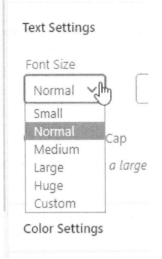

When you make a selection, the size of the font is displayed and can be edited manually for fine control over font size:

Go on and try these settings out.

The **Drop Cap** option can add some interest to your paragraph:

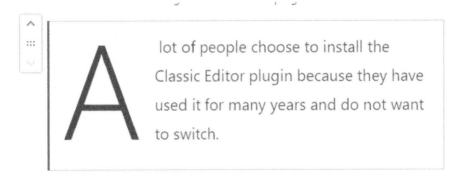

The paragraph block also has **Color Settings** that allow you to define the text and background color.

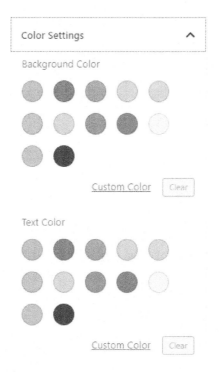

This gives you more flexibility in how your text appears on the page:

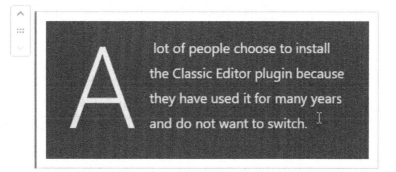

You will also find further formatting options in a toolbar at the top of the screen.

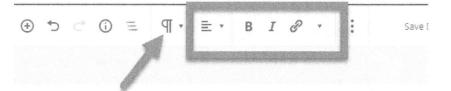

The formatting options available will obviously depend on the type of block you have selected. The above screenshot is for a paragraph block.

The first button in my screenshot shows that I have selected a paragraph block. Clicking that button allows you to convert the block type to a "compatible" alternative. Paragraph blocks can be converted to:

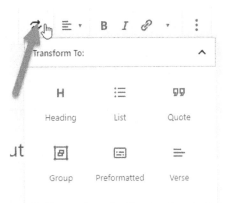

The other formatting options in the toolbar include alignment, bold, italic, link, inline code, inline image & strikethrough. These final three options are accessible through the drop-down menu button:

The alignment will affect the whole paragraph, but the other buttons will only be applied to the selected text within the paragraph.

The final menu button (three vertical dots) in the toolbar gives you a few block-related options:

	Save Draft	Preview
⚙ Hide Block Settings	Ctrl+Shift+,	
▮ Duplicate	Ctrl+Shift+D	
⊕ Insert Before	Ctrl+Alt+T	
⊕ Insert After	Ctrl+Alt+Y	
Edit as HTML		
Add to Reusable Blocks		
Group		
🗑 Remove Block	Shift+Alt+Z	

From this menu, you can duplicate the block, insert a block before or after the current one and edit as HTML. The final option allows you to delete the block.

But there are two features we skipped. Let's look at them.

Reusable Blocks

This is an interesting feature. It means you can save a block to be reused across your site. If you update the reusable block, you update it everywhere you use it.

To make a block reusable, click inside the block you want to use, and click the menu button. Select **Add to Reusable Blocks**. When you click that link, you will be asked to name your re-useable block before saving:

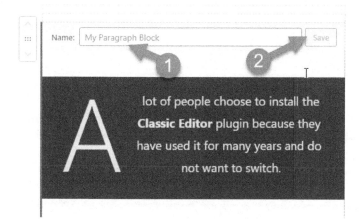

Once saved, your block becomes available in the block browser:

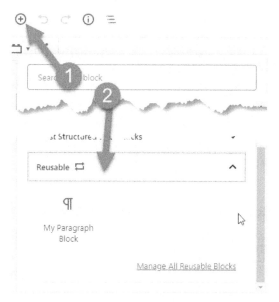

When you add it, you are adding an exact copy of the block you saved:

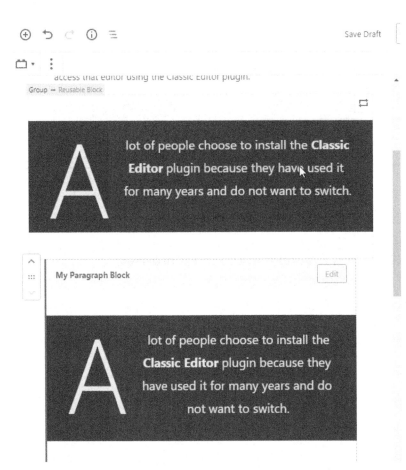

The thing is, you cannot edit this block without changing the original re-usable block as well, and every other instance of that block on your site. So where might re-useable blocks be useful? Examples would be calls to action, subscription forms, advertising banners, etc.

The Group block option creates a group containing your chosen block. You can then add more blocks to that group, which then can be saved as a re-useable group if you want.

This feature is fairly new at the time of writing this book and still a bit fiddly. However, it will be a powerful feature when it has matured a little.

The Image Block

There are a few ways we can add an image to our post. We know about the + button in the very top toolbar:

Perhaps a more intuitive method is to move your mouse towards the top of another block (not the page title) until you see a "+" appear in the middle of the block:

Gutenberg is the new block editor built into WordPress 5.0. It is a big change from the traditional classic editor, but fortunately you can still access that editor using the Classic Editor plugin.

I want an image to be aligned **Add block** paragraph. Let's do that now and we can see what options we have with the image block. All block properties can be found on the right hand side of the Gutenberg editor. So can the document properties.

Clicking that would open the block browser window so we can add any block we like above the current block. I'll select the image block:

Gutenberg is the new block editor built into WordPress 5.0. It is a big change from the traditional classic editor, but fortunately you can still access that editor using the Classic Editor plugin.

Image

Upload an image file, pick one from your media library, or add one with a URL.

Upload   Media Library

Insert from URL

I want an image to be aligned left in this paragraph. Let's do that now and we can see what options we have with the image block. All block

The image block is inserted above the paragraph block. As you can see, you can upload an image, choose an image from the Media Library, and choose an image URL to enter. Another option you have is to drag and drop an image from your computer into the block. Gutenberg will upload that image to the media library and insert it into your post.

You can add a caption to the image directly within the block.

When the image block is enabled, the context-sensitive menu at the top of your editor gives you some formatting options:

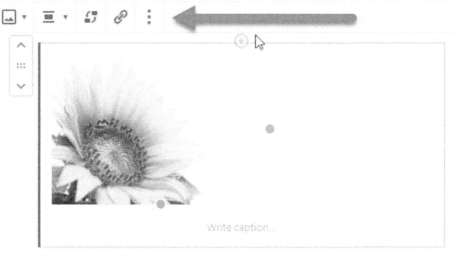

The first button allows you to switch the block to a different type, or select any of the available block styles.

The second button allows you to set the alignment of the image. This is really useful if you want the text to wrap around an image. Choose align left and see what happens:

access that editor using the Classic Editor plugin.

I want an image to be aligned left in this paragraph. Let's do that now and we can see what options we have with the image block. All block properties can be found on the right hand side of the Gutenberg editor. So can the document properties.

Write caption...

The next button is the Edit Image button. Clicking that is a quick way to go back and choose a different image:

The final button is to hyperlink the image to a URL, media file, or attachment page.

Make sure the image block is selected. On the right-hand side of the Gutenberg editor, the block properties refer to the image block:

The styles selection offers two alternatives. Try them.

Under image settings, you can add or edit the ALT text, image size, and dimensions. The advanced options give you some control over the CSS class of the image (advanced users).

The image block properties plus the formatting toolbar across the top, give you full control over your images. The same principles apply for all blocks.

Moving a Block in Gutenberg

Click inside the block you want to move.

A menu appears on the left side of the block:

The up and down arrow will move the block up or down one position.

There is also the grab handle in the middle of this menu.

Try this: Click on that handle and keep the mouse button pressed. Try dragging & dropping the block into a new position. Did it work?

The trick to getting this to work is to:

1. Click on the handle and keep the mouse button pressed in.
    2. Drag the image over to the right a little, until you see the horizontal position line:

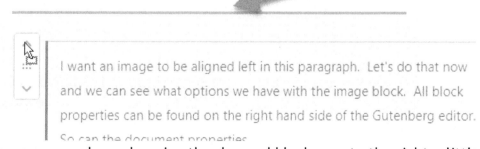

3. Now move the mouse up or down, keeping the dragged block over to the right a little. The horizontal position line will now move up and down, marking the position of the block if you drop it.

Practice dragging and dropping blocks until you get the hang of it.

Inserting Blocks in Between Existing Blocks

Each block in your post will display the toolbar at the top when you click into it. The right-hand button is the menu button that gives you the opportunity to insert a block before, or after, the current one.

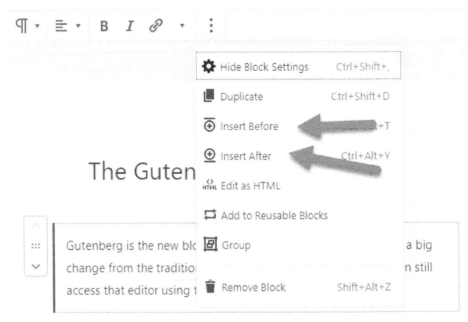

These options will insert a blank block which you can then work with:

The Gutenberg Editor

Gutenberg is the new block editor built into WordPress 5.0. It is a big change from the traditional classic editor, but fortunately you can still access that editor using the Classic Editor plugin.

Also, note that there are keyboard shortcuts for some items in the menu. For example, if you want to insert a block before an existing block, click the block and use the keyboard shortcut Ctrl+Alt+T (or the Mac equivalent).

We have already seen another way to insert one block between two others. Move your mouse over towards the top of the lower block and click the "+" to insert the block above.

Delete a Block

We have already seen this, but let's recap.

1. Select the block you want to remove.
2. From the menu at the top, click the button with three vertical dots.
3. Select **Remove Block**, or press SHIFT+ALT+Z on your keyboard.

So, we have the basics of adding, deleting and moving blocks. What blocks are actually available?

Available "Building" Blocks

The blocks menu is divided into groups of related blocks:

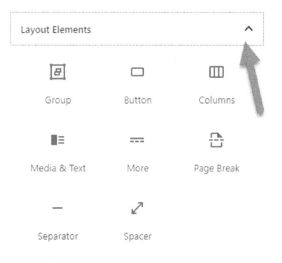

Just click the arrow on the right to unfold the set.

Here are a few that you will probably find yourself using regularly.

- Paragraph
- Image
- Heading
- List
- Quote
- Video
- Table
- Button
- Columns
- Separator
- Spacer

I won't go through all of the blocks that are available, as I want you to explore. It's easy. Just add a block and check out the top menu, and the block settings on the right of the Gutenberg editor. Change some settings to see how it affects the appearance of the block.

There are three blocks I would like to look at briefly.

The Table Block

One that is well-overdue is the table block. It's found in the formatting section, but it is easier to just search for it:

When you add a table block, you'll be asked for the row and column count. You can always edit this later by adding new columns or rows, but it is easier if you know now and can enter the precise dimensions.

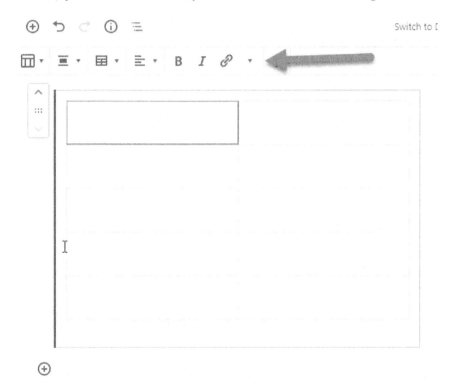

On clicking **Create Table**, you'll have a nicely formatted table awaiting data.

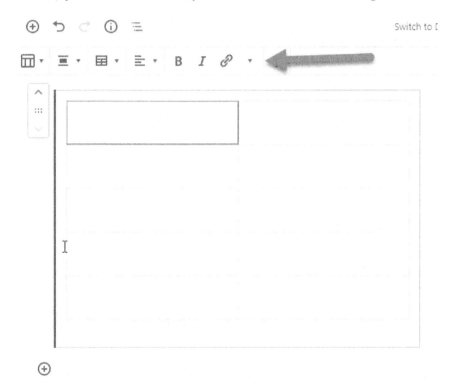

You can now enter nicely formatted tables of information.

Notice the toolbar at the top. The **Edit Table** button gives you the power to add or delete cells:

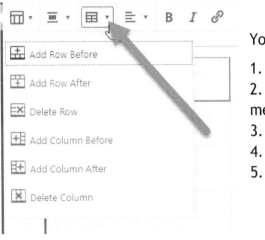

You can explore the table block for yourself. Try this:

1. Create a table and try adding data to it.
2. Try out the available "styles" (available from both the top menu and the block options).
3. Have a look at all of the table block properties.
4. Insert columns and rows to the table.
5. Delete columns and rows.

The Button Block

Another cool block is the **Button** block.

Insert a button block and click onto the text of the button (that says **Add text...**). Now type a caption for your button.

You can also specify a URL to link the button to. Maybe the button is a buy button and you need to link it to a PayPal URL.

Alternatively, you might want to link the button to an existing page on your site. Let's see how to do that by linking the button to the hello world post.

Start typing in some text from the title of the post you want to link to, and it should pop up for you to select:

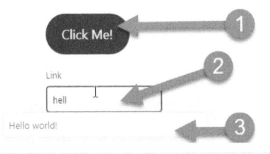

Select it and the URL of that post will be added to the URL box:

If you want the button to go to a webpage that is not part of your site, you can paste the URL directly into the URL box.

With the button block selected, have a look at the top toolbar. What styles are available? What are the other formatting options in the top toolbar? Try adding an inline image to your button to see what that does.

Take a look at the block properties:

Go through all of these options and see what you can change. You won't break anything.

The Columns Block

Another block that is nice to see is the columns block.

This block allows you to create layouts by positioning blocks within columns.

Add a columns block and you'll see this:

Choose the option that is closest to what you want to achieve. I'll choose the three-column layout:

I can now add blocks to each of the three columns by clicking on the + symbol in the middle of the column. What makes columns so powerful is that you can add more than one block to each column. In the following screenshot, I have added an image to the first column.

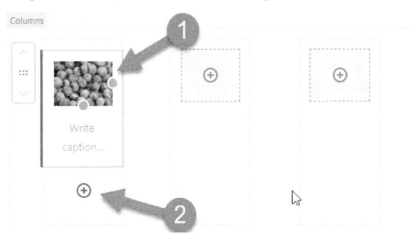

When I select that image, you can see the option to add another block underneath. If I move my mouse to the top of the image, I'd also be able to add a block above the image, but still inside the column.

With a column block inserted, have a look at the formatting options in the top toolbar.

Now have a look at the block properties.

If the column block is selected you can change the number of columns:

If an individual column is selected, you can change its width.

What happens if you select a block inside one of the columns?

Columns are quite cool!

Post (Document) Properties

As you work on your post or page, you have access to the document properties on the right.

These settings allow you to set the category of a post, add tags, set a featured image, create an excerpt, etc. We typically use these settings as we prepare a post for publishing. Let's go through the process.

The Process for Publishing a Post

Once you have written your post, there are a few other things you may want to do before hitting the publish button. Let's look at the typical workflow:

1. Write a post.
2. Choose a category.
3. Add tags.
4. Insert featured image.
5. Add an excerpt.
6. Publish or schedule.
7. Check/edit permalink (slug) of the post.

I'll assume you have created your post and you want to go through and publish it. Let's go through the steps:

1. Choose category

From the document settings, open the **Categories** section:

Categories

☑ Blog

☐ Toyota

   ☐ Auris

   ☐ Land Cruiser

   ☐ Prius

   ☐ Yaris

Add New Category

The default post category you chose when you set up the site will be checked. You can uncheck it if you want and choose a different category. You can also **Add a New Category** if you want, directly from the Gutenberg editor.

2. **Add tags**

In the **Tags** section, add a list of comma-separated words and phrases you want to use as tags. When you type a comma, the editor will add whatever came before the comma as a tag.

Tags

Add New Tag

| gutenberg ✖ |

Separate with commas or the Enter key.

3. **Insert featured image**

Featured images can be used by your theme e.g. as an image next to each post on an archive page (e.g.category or tag). Just click the **Set Featured Image** button to add an image from the media library (or upload).

4. **Add an excerpt**

Open the excerpt section and type in a paragraph about your post. This can be used by themes and/or plugins as a post summary, e.g. on recent post lists.

5. **Publish or schedule**

The Publish (or Update) button at the top can be used to publish your post or schedule it for future automatic publishing. We'll look at this in a little more detail in a moment. First, let's consider the last task in the publishing routine.

6. **Check/edit permalink (slug) of the post.**

When you publish a post, you'll have a new setting in the document properties – Permalink. This setting allows you to change the default file name for your post:

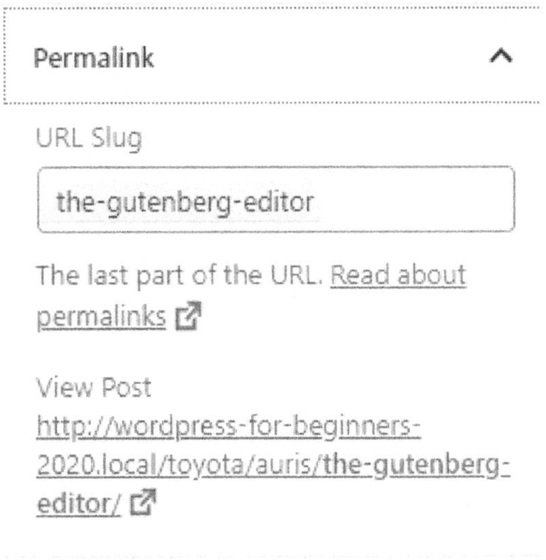

Permalink ︿

URL Slug

the-gutenberg-editor

The last part of the URL. Read about permalinks ⤢

View Post
http://wordpress-for-beginners-2020.local/toyota/auris/the-gutenberg-editor/ ⤢

You can see the URL slug in the screenshot above. This is created automatically by Gutenberg by taking the post title and stripping out invalid characters and converting spaces to hyphens. You are free to edit this. For SEO reasons, I would probably remove the "the" at the start. If you do make changes to the slug, make sure you click the update button to save changes.

So that's the routine for publishing a post. Let's have a look at the publishing options in a little more detail.

Publishing & Scheduling Posts in Gutenberg

The top item in the document properties is **Status & Visibility**. These options allow us to publish and schedule content, as well as to choose the post format (we saw post formats earlier) and even send the post to trash.

At the top of this block of settings, you'll see the word **Public**. This is the default setting and means the post will be visible to anyone that comes to your site. If you click the Public link, you'll see that you can also set posts to **Private**, or **Password Protected**.

These are self-explanatory so read the brief description of each.

Under the **Visibility** settings, you can see the **Publish** settings. With a new post, the default is "Immediately":

If you click the Immediately link, you'll get a popup calendar allowing you to schedule the post's publication to a future date. When that date and time arrives, the post will be automatically published by WordPress.

Once you've selected when to publish, click the **Publish** button at the top. You'll be asked to confirm the publication settings:

When you are sure, click the **Publish** button again.

The post will then be published at the selected date and time. Using the HTML Editor to Edit Your Post

There may be times when you want to edit your post in raw HTML code. To do this, click on the ellipsis menu button, top right of the Gutenberg editor:

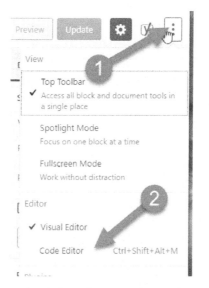

Currently, the **Visual Editor** is selected. It's what we have been using so far. If you choose **Code Editor** instead, you can view/edit the entire post as HTML code.

The Gutenberg Editor

```
<!-- wp:paragraph -->
<p>Gutenberg is the new block editor built into WordPress 5.0.  It is a big
change from the traditional classic editor, but fortunately you can still
access that editor using the Classic Editor plugin.</p>
<!-- /wp:paragraph -->

<!-- wp:group -->
<div class="wp-block-group"><div class="wp-block-group__inner-container">
<!-- wp:group -->
<div class="wp-block-group"><div class="wp-block-group__inner-container">
<!-- wp:block {"ref":45} /--></div></div>
<!-- /wp:group --></div></div>
<!-- /wp:group -->

<!-- wp:block {"ref":45} /-->
```

You can make changes in the HTML editor and save changes as required. You can revert back to the **Visual Editor** at any time by clicking that item in the same menu.

Yoast SEO Settings for the Post

When we installed the Yoast SEO plugin, it added a panel to the add post (and add page) screen.

If you scroll down a little, you should come across the **Yoast SEO** section.

Yoast SEO

    ● SEO   😊 Readability   ⊰ Social

Focus keyphrase ❓

Snippet Preview   ⌄

● SEO analysis   ⌄

✛ Add related keyphrase   ⌄

Cornerstone content   ⌄

Advanced   ⌄

This Yoast SEO box looks very similar to the ones we saw for the category and tag pages. Some of the more powerful features of this plugin can be found on the **Advanced** tab.

Advanced   ⌃

Allow search engines to show this Post in search results?

Default for Posts, currently: Yes   ▾

Should search engines follow links on this Post?
◉ Yes   ○ No

Meta robots advanced

× Site-wide default: None

Advanced `meta` robots settings for this page.

Canonical URL

The canonical URL that this page should point to. Leave empty to default to permalink. Cross domain canonical supported too.

These settings give us fine control over how the search engines will deal with this post. We can use these settings to override the global settings for the site. This is powerful. With this fine level of control, we can treat every post and page on our site differently if we want to.

The top setting allows us to show/hide a post from the search engines. By default, all posts will be indexed by the search engines. If we don't want a post indexed and visible in the search engines, we can select **No** from the drop-down box (which sets the page to noindex for those that know what this means). However, this would be most unusual for posts.

The next setting is whether search engines should follow links in this post. The default is yes, but we can set them to No (which is a nofollow tag for those that know what this means). I don't recommend changing this unless you know what you are doing.

The **Meta Robots Advanced** allows us to set a few other Meta tags on our pages. Click on the edit box where it currently says **Site-wide default: None** and a drop-down box appears with options you can set:

Meta robots advanced

> × Site-wide default: None

> Site-wide default: None

> None

> No Image Index

> No Archive

> No Snippet

canonical supported too.

No Image Index is useful if you don't want the search engines to index the images on your page. Indexed images can be easily found within the image search on Google, and pirated.

No Archive tag tells Google not to store a cached copy of your page

No Snippet tells Google not to show a description under your Google listing (nor will it show a cached link in the search results).

The only option you may want to add occasionally is the **No Archive** option, but only in very special circumstances. There are times when we don't want Google to keep an archive (cached version), of a page. By setting the post as **No Archive** we are preventing the search engines from keeping a backup of the page.

Why might you want to do this?

Well, maybe you have a limited offer on your site and you don't want people seeing it after the offer has finished. If the page was archived, it is technically possible for someone to go in and see the last cached page at Google, which will still show your previous offer.

Before we go any further, I want to disable a couple of features of the Yoast SEO plugin. These are SEO analysis and Readability. It's up to you if you want to keep them enabled. Some people like the idea of a plugin that can give SEO recommendations, but in reality, the plugin is just counting keywords, so you can optimize your page around a single keyword. That used to work a few years back, but optimizing a page for a single keyword today will get your page kicked out of Google. The readability score is just a feature I don't use.

To deactivate these, click on **SEO** in the sidebar menu of the dashboard.

On the **General** page, click on the **Features** tab.

You can now switch these features off:

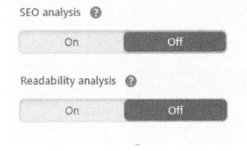

If you decide to keep these enabled, be aware that you'll have the extra information relating to these features in your dashboard. They won't be in my screenshots from now on.

Editing Posts

At some point after writing a post, you may want to go in and edit or update it. This is an easy process. Just click on **All Posts** in the **Posts** menu. It will open a screen with a list of posts on your site.

In the screenshot, you can see that I have three posts on the site. The top one is scheduled, the second one is published, and the third one is a draft.

You can view just the published, just the scheduled, or just the draft posts, by clicking on the item in the menu at the top. You can also view any posts you sent to Trash as long as the trash has not been emptied.

What if you had a lot of posts and needed to find one?

There are two ways of doing this. One is from within your Dashboard using the available search and filtering tools. The other method is one I'll show you later and involves visiting your site while you are logged into the Dashboard.

For now, let's look at three ways we can find posts from within the Dashboard.

Method 1: Perhaps the easiest way of all is to use the **Search Posts** feature. Type in a keyword phrase you know is in the title and then click the **Search Posts** button.

Posts Add New

All (3) | Published (1) | Scheduled (1) | Draft (1) | Trash (2) | Cornerstone content (0)

Search Posts

Bulk Actions ∨ Apply   All dates ∨   All Categories ∨ Filter   3 items

☐ Title   Author   Categories   Tags   💬   Date   ⬑

Once the list of matching posts is displayed, mouseover the one you want to edit and click Edit from the popup menu. An even easier way is to just click the title of the post. This takes you back to the same editor screen you used when first creating the post. Make your changes in there and just click the **Update** button to save your modifications.

Method 2: If you know what month you wrote the post, you could show all posts from that month by selecting the month from the **All Dates** drop-down box. Once selected, click the **Filter** button.

Method 3: You can also search for a post by showing just those posts within a certain category. Select the desired category from the **All Category** drop-down box. Once selected, click the **Filter** button.

Revisions

Whenever you make changes to a post, WordPress keeps a record (archive), of those changes. You'll see the revisions section in the document properties (as long as you have made changes to the page over time, and saved those changes):

Click on the Revisions section to open it out:

The slider at the top allows you to scroll between the various revisions. As you move through the revisions, you'll see the date and time that revision was saved.

In the main window, you'll see differences between the two revisions highlighted. E.g. I change the title from "The Gutenberg Editor", to "A Gutenberg Editor". Here is the revision screen:

The latest version is on the right, the previous version is on the left. As you scroll back through revisions, you'll always see two versions. On the right will be the version that was saved on that date. On the left was the previous version.

At any time, if you want to revert to a previous version, click the **Restore This Revision** button. The version of the right of the revisions screen will be the one restored. At the same time, a new revision is created for the "latest" version of the post.

Why Use Revisions?

Suppose you are working on a post and delete a paragraph or change an image. Later, you ask yourself "why did I delete that?". With revisions, you can revert to previous versions of your post with a few mouse clicks.

Making it Easy for Visitors to Socially Share Your Content

Having great content on your site is one thing but getting people to see it is something else.

One of the ways people find a website is through search engines. If we rank well enough for a particular search term, the web searcher may land on our page.

Another way people can find our content is via social media channels. Places like Facebook and Twitter are good examples. To make this more likely, we need to install a social sharing plugin on the site. A social sharing plugin will add buttons to the website that allow people to share the content they are reading with their followers. Social sharing buttons make sharing easy, and therefore more likely.

There are several good social sharing plugins and I do recommend you look around to find one that matches the design of your website. However, to get you started, let's install my current favorite.

Go to **Add New** in the **Plugins** menu. Search for **Grow by Mediavine** and look for this one:

Install and activate the plugin.

This plugin was previously called Social Pug. At the time of writing this book, the plugin did still use that name in the settings for the plugin. Have a look in the sidebar menu:

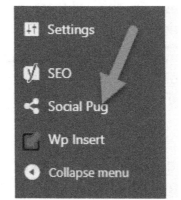

NOTE: Since they have changed the name of the plugin in the plugin repository, they may eventually get around to changing the name used in the sidebar menu. If you don't see Social Pug, look for Grow or Mediavine.

Click that menu to be taken to the settings screen.

This plugin offers you two options for displaying social sharing buttons.

Social Share Tools

Floating Sidebar	Inline Content
Settings	Settings

These are both enabled in the screenshot above. You can use one system or both. Activate or deactivate using the slider next to each option.

The floating sidebar will create a panel on your web page, which "floats" down the side of your content and is always visible. The inline content option will insert the buttons before and/or after the article on your web page.

Before the social sharing buttons appear on your site, you need to tell the plugin which social accounts you want to include. Click on the "cog" button that appears:

The first thing you'll need to do is select which social sharing networks you want to offer your visitors. Facebook, Twitter, and Pinterest are selected by default.

Click the **Select Networks** button, and place a checkmark next to the networks you want:

Social Networks

✔ **f Facebook**   ✔ **🐦 Twitter**   ✔ **𝓟 Pinterest**

in LinkedIn   **✉ Email**   **🖨 Print**

Apply Selection

Click the **Apply Selection** button.

The networks will now appear on the settings screen, and you can re-order these by dragging them up or down using the "handle" on the left. You can also delete a network by clicking the "X Remove" link on the right.

Below you'll see some display settings. I'll leave you to explore these options.

When you are ready, make sure that **Post** is checked under the **Post type display settings**. If you want to include sharing buttons on pages, make sure that is checked.

Post Type Display Settings

☑ Post   Page

Save Changes

Click **Save Changes.**

If you are using both inline and floating buttons, you need to set them both up separately.

If you visit your site, you should now see the social sharing buttons on posts (and pages if you enabled that). If you chose floating sidebar, it looks like this:

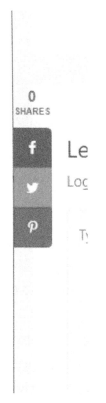

If you chose the inline content, it will look like this:

A Gutenberg Editor

Leave a Comment / Auris / By Andy

Sharing is caring!

Gutenberg is the new block editor built into WordPress 5.0. It is a big change from the traditional classic editor, but fortunately you can still access that editor using the Classic Editor plugin.

Obviously, yours won't look exactly like mine as it depends on the settings you chose.

Other Social Share Plugins

Over the years I have tried lots of social sharing plugins. Some work great, while others only seem to work on some websites and not others. If you find Grow by Mediavine does not work properly on *your* site, just search for "social share" in the **Add Plugins** screen, and try some.

Tasks to Complete

1. Enter a post. It doesn't have to be a real post and you can always delete it afterward. I just want you to feel comfortable using the WYSIWYG editor. Add text and an image, and then play around with the image alignment and settings.

2. Publish your post and go to your site to see how it looks in your web browser.

3. Go back and edit the post and resave (to create a revision). Repeat this a few times making changes to the post each time you do.

4. Now scroll to the bottom of the page and look at the revisions section. Check out the differences between two revisions of your post. Use the slider to scroll through the revisions. Try reinstating an earlier version and then change it back again.

5. Install a social sharing plugin and set it up to suit your needs.

Differences with Pages

As we discussed earlier, pages are different from posts. On the Add/Edit Page screen, it all looks very similar, but there are a few notable omissions – namely no categories or tags! There is also no box to add an excerpt.

We do, however, have a couple of options for pages that are not found in posts – Page Attributes:

These settings allow you to set up parent-child relationships between your pages. It's not something that most beginners will need, so I won't cover that in this book.

Tasks to Complete

1. Go and look at the page edit screen. Note the page attributes box.

Internal Linking of Posts

One of the best ways of keeping visitors on your site is to interlink your web pages. There are a few ways of doing this.

The basic way to add a link in your content is to highlight the word or phrase that you want to use as the link's text and then click on the link button in the toolbar.

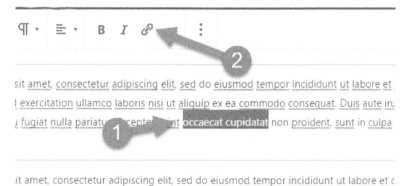

A popup box will appear next to the highlighted word or phrase. If you want to link to a webpage on a different website, paste the URL into the box.

If you want to link to a post/page on your website, type in part of the title of the webpage and WordPress will find it for you:

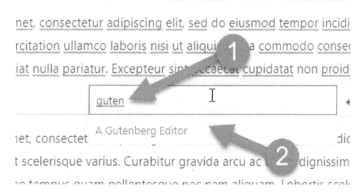

Click the post/page in the list that you want to link to. This sets the URL in the URL box. To accept the link, you can click the "Apply" button. However, before you do, click the downward arrow button to the right of the apply button to get one important option:

Open in New Tab does what it says. This is something I recommend if you are linking to another website. That way, your visitor will remain on your site, and the link target will open in a new browser window for them.

When you are happy, click the **Apply** button and the link will appear in the text. If you click the link to select it, you'll see a little pencil icon which you can click if you need to edit the link:

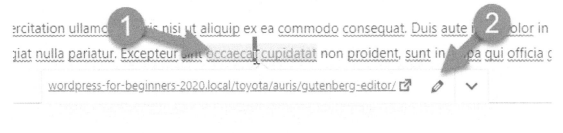

There is also a useful button right next to the URL.

This will open that URL in a new tab so you can check the URL is correct.

When you have selected a link, if you look at the toolbar at the top, the link icon has changed.

It is now an "unlink" button, which you can use to remove the hyperlink if you want to.

OK, that's the 100% manual way of interlinking your web pages.

Related Posts With YARPP

One way I recommend you inter-link your content is with a plugin called **Yet Another Related Posts**. This plugin allows you to set up a "Related Articles" section at the end of your posts. This will automatically create links to related articles on your site.

Go to the **Add New** Plugin screen and search for **yarpp**.

Yet Another Related Posts Plugin (YARPP)

Install Now

Display a list of related posts on your site based on a powerful unique algorithm. Optionally, earn money by including sponsored content.

By YARPP

More Details

★ ★ ★ ★ ☆ (368)

200,000+ Active Installations

Last Updated: 3 weeks ago

✓ Compatible with your version of WordPress

Install and activate the plugin.

You will now find the YARPP settings in the main settings menu:

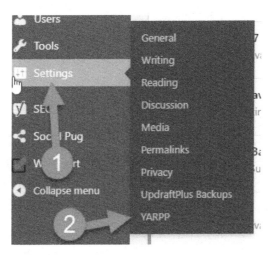

Click on **YARPP** so we can set this up.

At the top of the YARPP settings, is "The Pool". The pool is the set of posts that can be used for building a related articles section. If you decide you don't want any posts from a particular category showing up in related article sections, you can exclude that category here by checking the box next to that category. You can do the same by Tag.

There is also an option to limit the age of posts in the pool, only including posts from the previous X days, weeks, or months.

I am going to leave the pool defaults as they are.

If you think you won't be changing these settings, you can hide "The Pool" by unchecking the option in the **Screen Options.**

The next settings on the page are the "Relatedness" options. This defines how closely related an article needs to be, to be shown as a "related post".

I recommend you leave the relatedness options with their default values. The only change I make on smaller sites is to change the Match Threshold to a 1. On larger sites, a 2 is OK.

Next up are the **Display options for your website.**

There is plenty of scope for playing around here as well, including using your own template, but we are going to use the default settings, with one exception. Place a checkmark next to **Show excerpt?** This will give our related posts a description, which is taken from the post excerpt. When you check that box, a few more options appear. Change Excerpt length to 50 (I recommend that you experiment with this setting).

Ok, that is all we are changing. Scroll to the bottom and click **Save Changes.**

You will now have a related posts section at the end of every post on the site. You probably won't see much yet because you don't have content on the site. Here is what I see at the end of my post on this demo site:

However, as you start adding content, the related posts section will start to populate with recommendations for your visitors.

Here is an example of a related posts section on one of my sites using this plugin.

Related Posts:

1. January 2016 Google Algorithm Updates
   January 2016 saw some major updates in Google, with wild swings in the rankings of many sites. What do we know about this update?...

2. Google Penguin, and other Google News
   Google's Penguin 4.0 is coming soon. What can you expect and how can you get ready for it?...

3. Finding Hot Niches
   If you have ever had problems identifying niches, or you have built a site that you thought would be profitable, and its wasn't, then Gary Harvey might have the answer with his latest offering – "Finding Hot Niches". This site is dedicated to showing you the best resources for researching...

This "related posts" section was on an article about search engine optimization on my ezSEONews.com site. Can you see the benefits? People who are reading the main SEO article are shown other articles that are related to what they've just been reading about. It gives us another chance to keep the visitor on our site.

We have looked at two ways we can inter-link our content. Firstly, we can manually create links in the content. Secondly, we can use a plugin like YARPP to show related posts to our visitors.

The last option I like to use is a plugin that I can set up to control internal linking on an automated basis, but without losing control over the linking.

I have written an article on internal site linking using this plugin. If you are interested, you should read that article here:

https://ezseonews.com/backlinks/internal-linking-seo/

Tasks to Complete

1. Go and edit an existing post or create one for this exercise. Manually add a few links on this page. They can be links to pages on your site, or another website entirely.

2. Open the page in a web browser and check that the links you added work properly.

3. Install YARPP and configure it. As you add more content to your website, check out the related posts section (found at the end of every post).

The Homepage of Your Site - Blog or Static?

WordPress is a tool that was originally created as a blogging platform (publishing date-related content as posts). The way in which WordPress handles these posts by default is to post them on the homepage, with the latest post at the top of that page.

In the settings, we saw that we could define how many posts to include on a page with the default set at 10. That means the last 10 posts published on the site will show up on the homepage in chronological order, with the latest post at the top and older posts below. As you post more content on the site, the older posts scroll off the bottom of the homepage and are replaced by the newer ones at the top.

If that is the type of site you want, then that's fine. You can ignore this section and leave things at their default settings.

Personally, I like to create a homepage that always displays the content I want my visitors to see on the homepage. In fact, I create a "homepage article" describing the main point of the site and helping visitors with navigation.

The good news is that creating this type of "static" homepage in WordPress is easy.

Create a WordPress "page" (not a post) and write your homepage content. Publish the page and then go to the **Reading** settings inside the **Settings** menu. Do not continue until your homepage article is published.

At the top of the screen, there are two radio buttons with **Your latest posts** selected as default. You need to select the **Static page** option.

Two drop-down boxes will appear. The top one labeled **Homepage** is the one we are interested in. Click on the drop-down box and select the page you created with your homepage article.

I've called mine "My Homepage" to make it clear in this example that this will be the homepage. You should give your homepage article a useful, real title because it will appear as the headline at the top of your homepage.

At the bottom of your page, click on the **Save Changes** button.

OK, you are all set. Go to your homepage and you'll see the article you selected is now your homepage.

You can see how easy it is to create this type of static page for the homepage of your website.

No matter how many posts you add to your site, that homepage "article" will not change (unless you change it).

OK, I hear your question.

"If the homepage just shows the same article, how are people going to find all my other web pages?"

Well, that's where the website navigation system comes in. We'll look at that next.

Tasks to Complete

1. If you want your homepage to show the same article, create a PAGE with that article. Edit the **Reading** settings to show that page on your **Homepage**.

Navigation Menus

To add or edit a navigation menu in WordPress, go to **Menus** inside the **Appearance** menu.

Let's design a menu for our website. In it, we'll add links to the legal pages we created – Contact, Privacy Policy, and Terms.

Add a name in the **Menu Name** box, and click the **Create Menu** button:

I've called my menu "Legal Menu" to reflect its purpose. This makes things easier when you have multiple menus and you are trying to decide which one is which.

On the left of the screen, you'll have a section that lists all Pages, Posts, Custom Links, Categories, etc. Pull down the **Screen Options** and check Tags as well.

You can now add any post, page, category page or tag page to the menu.

Currently, the Pages section is expanded. You can see three tabs at the top: **Most Recent**, **View All** and **Search**. These will help you find a specific page, so you can insert it into the menu.

To expand a different section, simply click on the section. E.g. When I click on **Posts**, Pages collapse, and Posts open:

Add menu items

Pages	▼
Posts	▲

Most Recent   View All   Search

☐ One for the future
☐ A Gutenberg Editor

☐ Select All   Add to Menu

Custom Links   ▼

Since we want to add legal pages, click on the Pages section to expand it. We want the privacy policy, terms, and contact. If you can see them all on the **Most Recent** screen, check the box next to each one. If you don't see them all listed in most recent, click on view all, and you will find them there.

With all three checked, click the **Add to Menu** button:

You will see all three added to the menu on the right-hand side of the screen:

Menu structure

Menu Name Legal Menu   Save Menu

Drag each item into the order you prefer. Click the arrow on the right of the item to reveal additional configuration options.

Terms and Conditions   Page ▼

Contact   Page ▼

Privacy Policy   Page ▼

Menu Settings

Auto add pages ☐ Automatically add new top-level pages to this menu

Display location ☐ Primary Menu
                   ☐ Footer Menu

Delete Menu   Save Menu

If you move your mouse over one of the items in the menu, the cursor changes:

Contact   Page ▼

Terms and Conditions   Page ▼

Privacy Policy   Page ▼

This cursor indicates that the item can be dragged and dropped. Click and drag it up or down to re-order the items in the menu. I want Terms at the top, then privacy, and contact at the bottom.

Under these three menu items are two other options:

Menu Settings

Auto add pages ☐ Automatically add new top-level pages to this menu

Display location ☐ Primary Menu
                   ☐ Footer Menu

Delete Menu   Save Menu

The **Auto Add Pages** option will automatically add new pages you create on the site to this menu. That typically isn't something we want, so leave it unchecked.

The second option defines the location of the menu within the theme. The Astra theme has two locations assigned to menus. One is the primary menu, and the other is the Footer menu.

The Primary menu is across the top of the site, to the right of the header. Check **Primary Menu** and then **Save Menu**. Now go and check out your website.

WordPress for Beginners 2020   Terms and Conditions   Privacy Policy   Contact

Meta

My Homepage   Site Admin

Log out

Entries feed

Comments feed

WordPress.org

You can see the menu has been added to the top right. The Astra theme is responsive, so if you resize your browser window and make it smaller, the menu will collapse to a "Menu" button, and clicking the button will open the menu:

Press for Beginners 2020   ≡

Try it. Resize your browser until the menu button appears, then click it to see your menu displayed. Increase the size of your browser again to see the horizontal menu re-appear.

Menu Hierarchy

It is possible to create hierarchical drop-down menus. In other words, each item in the menu can have a parent or child type relationship.

Using my menu above to illustrate, if I drag the privacy policy a little to the right, it becomes indented under the first one. Repeating this for the contact link result in this:

Terms	Page ▼
Privacy Policy *sub item*	Page ▼
Contact *sub item*	Page ▼

Save the menu and then visit your site again.

The menu will now just show the "parent" item, in this case, **Terms and Conditions**:

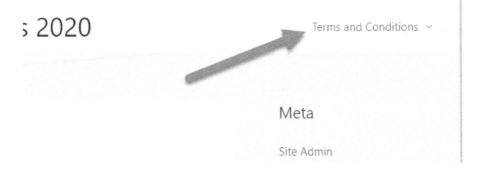

Moving your mouse over **Terms and Conditions** will open the menu:

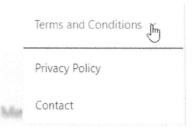

This technique can be used to tidy up big menus with lots of items, but it does not make sense to do so in the above example. It's easy enough to fix though, just un-indent those items.

On the **Menus** screen, you'll probably have noticed two tabs at the top – **Edit Menus** and **Manage Locations**. The Edit Menus screen is the one we have been working in to create this menu. The Manage Locations screen is there to make it easier to manage multiple menus and place them in the predefined locations within the theme. Since Astra has two menu locations, you can see them both listed here, and you can choose which menu to insert into each, by selecting from the drop-down box:

OK, switch back to the **Edit Menus** tab.

One other type of link that can be added to a menu is a custom link. You can see it listed there on the left. This allows you to link to any URL you like, and add that link to the menu.

To create a custom link, add the URL of the page you want to link to and the link text you want to appear, then click **Add to Menu**.

Custom Links ▲

URL   https://google.com

Link Text   Google

             Add to Menu

The link will be added to the menu.

Terms and Conditions	Page ▼
Privacy Policy	Page ▼
Contact	Page ▼
Google	Custom Link ▼

Custom links are labeled as such. Posts will be labeled as Post, and pages are obviously labeled as Page.

You may have noticed that each link in the menu has a little arrow on the far right. Click it to expand the options for that link:

Terms and Conditions   Page ▲

Navigation Label
Terms and Conditions

Move *Down one*

Original: *Terms and Conditions*

Remove | Cancel

At the bottom, you can **Remove** a menu item.

The default link settings only provide the options shown above, as some are hidden. Open the **Screen Options** and check the options for **Link Target** and **Link Relationship (XFN)**.

You will now see two new items in the options:

The **Link target** creates the checkbox so you can choose to have menu links open in a new tab.

The **Link Relationship** allows you to add nofollow tags to your links. If you don't know what these are, don't worry. Simply put, the nofollow tag tells a search engine that a page you are linking to is not important. I often use these on links to my legal pages, like this:

Edit an Existing Menu

There will be times when you want to edit an existing menu. This is straightforward enough. Go to **Menus** in the **Appearance** menu.

If you only have one menu, that is the one you will see. If you have more than one menu created, use the drop-down box to choose the menu you want to edit:

Click the **Select** button to switch to that menu and edit.

Navigation Menu Widgets

Any menu you create can be added to a sidebar (or any widgetized area) using the navigation menu widget.

First, let's **Create a new menu:**

We create it the same way. Give your menu a meaningful name (I am calling mine **Sidebar Menu**) and click the **Create Menu** button.

I'll just add a couple of posts to the menu using the posts selector and then save my new menu.

OK, head back to **Widgets** in the **Appearance** menu.

When you get there, drag a **Navigation Menu** widget into the **Main Sidebar** area:

Add a title and select the menu from the drop-down box.

Save the widget, then check out the sidebar on your homepage.

Here is mine:

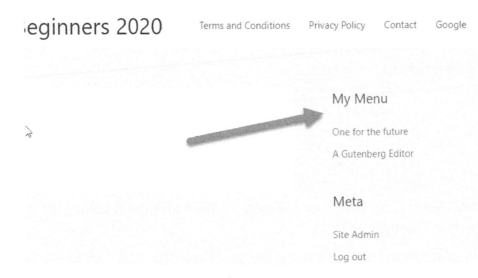

You can create navigation menus for all kinds of things. These may be top review pages or important tag pages. The point is this; custom menus give you the flexibility you need as you design and develop your website.

Tasks to Complete

1. Go and experiment with Navigation Menus.
2. Create a menu with a "Home" link (custom link to homepage URL) and links to the "legal" pages on your site.
3. Add the menu to a widgetized area of your site.

Viewing Your Site While Logged In

Something special happens when you are visiting your website while logged into the Dashboard.

Earlier, when we were looking at the User Profile, we made sure an option was checked – **Show Toolbar when viewing site**. Let's see what happens with that option enabled.

Log in to your dashboard and then open your website in another tab of your web browser. What you'll see is a very useful "ribbon" across the top of your website:

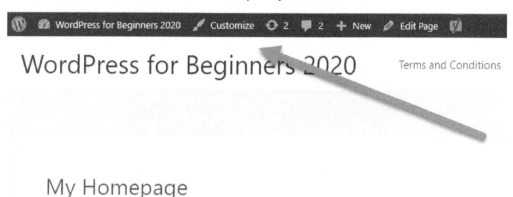

This ribbon gives you access to some important WordPress features. For example, if you want to edit a page or post on your website, you can visit your website, find the post, then click on the edit post link in the ribbon bar (you can see it in the screenshot above). That will open the post in the WordPress Dashboard ready for editing.

The ribbon is very useful as you browse your site. If you find errors, just click the **Edit Page/Post** link, fix the issue(s), and then click the **Update** button.

Some items in the menu have drop-down options. Mouseover your site name on the left, and you'll have links to:

These links will take you directly to those areas of the Dashboard. There is also a quick way to add new content to your site. Mouseover the **New** item to quickly add a new post, page, media item or user:

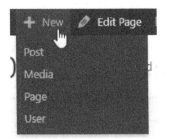

If you installed the Yoast SEO plugin, that adds a drop-down menu to the toolbar too, offering quick SEO links. I'll leave you to explore those.

Finally, on the right, if you mouse over your name, you'll get this menu:

These options are self-explanatory.

The ribbon has a couple of useful indicators too. If you have any updates that need installing, the update indicator will tell you:

If you mouse over this, it will tell you what needs updating. In my case, it's two plugins. Clicking the update indicator will take you to the **Update** section of the Dashboard.

There is also a speech bubble that represents comments awaiting moderation. If there are comments waiting, the speech bubble will tell you how many. In my case, I have 2 comments awaiting moderation:

Clicking the speech bubble will open the Dashboard on the moderation screen.

Tasks to Complete

1. Log in to your site.
2. Open the site in a new tab in your browser.
3. Mouseover, then click every option in the ribbon bar at the top. See what these links do and where they take you when you click them.

WordPress Security

WordPress has often been criticized for being too easy to hack. There have been a lot of cases where people have lost their WordPress site after a hacker gained access to it and wreaked havoc. Several years ago, one of my sites got hacked so badly that I just deleted the whole thing and let the domain expire. At that time, I didn't have a reliable backup system in place.

We set up a plugin earlier called UpdraftPlus. That is creating backups for us, and it is a great start.

Another layer of protection is to **always upgrade WordPress** (and plugins) as soon as there is a new update available.

The WordPress team fix security leaks as soon as they are found. Therefore, if your Dashboard says there is a WordPress upgrade, install it as soon as possible to make sure your copy has all the bug fixes and/or security patches.

Finally, the All-in-One Security plugin we mentioned earlier is something I install on all my own sites. Do watch this video tutorial for a basic installation and setup of that plugin:

https://ezseonews.com/WordPresstutorials/all-in-one-wp-security-firewall/

For those that want more guidance on security, I have a full video course on the topic of WordPress Security and how to make sure your site is virtually hack-proof. If you want more details on that, please visit:

https://ezseonews.com/udemy

That page lists all my courses, so just look for the WordPress Security course if that is the one that interests you.

Tasks to Complete

1. Make sure UpdraftPlus is making regular backups of your site and preferably storing them in the cloud, e.g. on Dropbox.
2. Always keep WordPress (and plugins) up to date.
3. Watch the free All in One Security Firewall video from the link above and consider setting it up to secure your website.

Monitoring Website Traffic

Every Webmaster wants to know how many visitors their site is getting and how those people are finding their pages (search engines, social media channels, etc.).

Fortunately, there are good (and free) solutions to give you this information.

The tool I use on my own sites is called **Google Analytics**, but it is complex and perhaps overkill for someone just starting out. I'd, therefore, recommend you check out a free service like "Get Clicky":

http://clicky.com/

I won't go into details on setting this up, but it is straightforward. You'll need to sign up for a free account and then install tracking on your website. This plugin can help with that:

Once integrated into your site, Clicky will monitor your visitors. You'll get information about where they come from and what they do on your site.

As your site grows, I'd highly recommend you investigate Google Analytics and make the switch. It's the best free tool out there and gives a wealth of information about your visitors.

Tasks to Complete

1. Install web analytics on your site. An easy option for beginners is to use the free services over at **Get Clicky**.

2. Install the "Clicky by Yoast" plugin and configure it as per the installation instructions on the plugin site.

3. Log in to your Get Clicky account and explore the reports and options. Use their help if needed.

4. When you have time, look into Google Analytics.

Types of WordPress Websites

A lot of people think of WordPress as a blogging tool. It's true that you can create a blog with Wordpress, but it's not limited to that type of site. In this section, I want to show you three typical ways in which WordPress is used in the real world. We'll look at a typical WordPress website, a blog, and a business site.

I'll start by introducing these three site structures. At the end of the section, I'll give you a link to go and watch videos of these structures being created in WordPress.

A Typical WordPress Website

The typical WordPress website has a static homepage and number of posts, organized into categories. There will be a few WordPress pages for contact, privacy, etc. The site may or may not have a separate blog. Here is that structure:

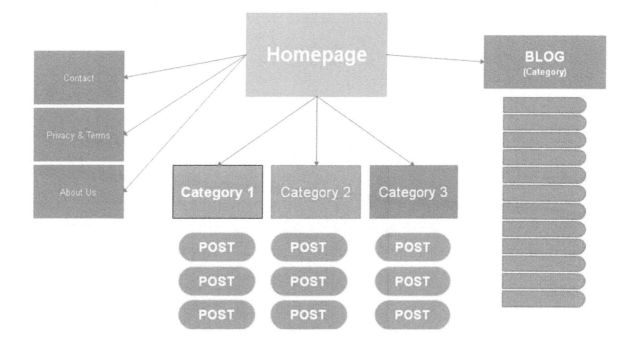

A Blog

A typical blog is based on WordPress posts to create an organized, chronological sequence of web pages. The homepage of a blog is typically just a list of all the posts in chronological order. However, you can also create a blog-style site that has a static homepage. WordPress pages will only be used for contact, privacy, etc. Here is that structure:

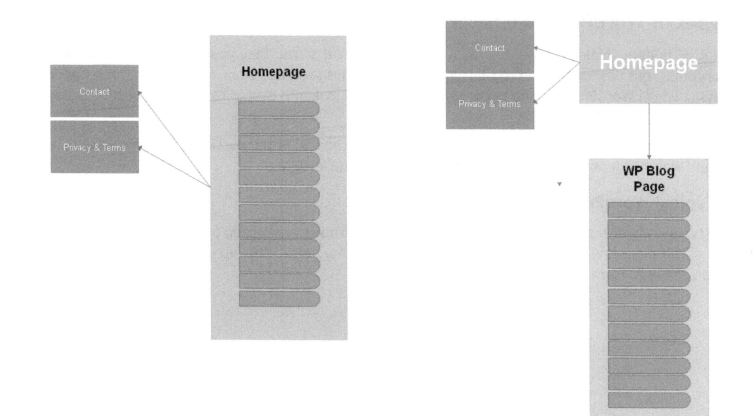

A Business Site

A business site typically uses WordPress Pages for the main site content, rather than posts. However, it is common for business sites to also include a blog, where the business can make announcements. Here is that site structure:

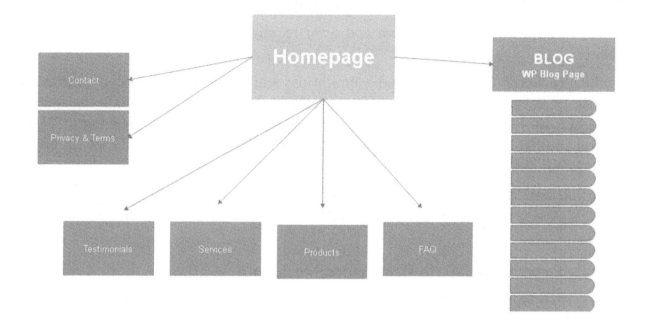

Using the knowledge you have gained from this book, you could quite easily replicate these three types of site yourself. However, to give you that extra helping hand, I have recorded a video for each of these site structures, showing how to set each one up inside your dashboard.

You can watch the videos here:

https://ezseonews.com/wp4b-tutorials

Appendix I - Moving a Site from WordPress.com to WordPress.org

So, you've outgrown WordPress.com and want to move your content to a hosted WordPress.org website?

Switching to WordPress.org will remove limitations and give you a lot of new features and freedom. Fortunately making the switch is not too difficult. I should warn you though that not everything is moved across. Your content and images will be, as will categories and tags. That means the important stuff. You will need to change themes, add plugins, and generally set up, but your content will be safe.

Before you start the move, you need to have web hosting and a domain name. We covered hosting and registrars earlier in this book, so go back and make sure you have the domain and hosting set up.

Step 1 - Export Your Data from WordPress.com

Log in to your WordPress.com website and click on the **Tools** menu in the left sidebar, then **Export**.

The screen loads with an **Export All** button, but also a down arrow that opens a panel with more options:

Export Your Content
Your content on WordPress.com is always yours.

Export your content

Export all (or specific) text content (pages, posts, feedback) from your site.

Export All

Export media library

Download all the media library files (images, videos, audio and documents) from your site.

Download

Click on the down arrow to open up the export options.

You'll see that you can define which posts or which pages you want to export. If you want to export all, then click the **Export All** button.

You will get a message saying the export was successful and a link was sent to your email address. However, you can also click the **Download** link to get the exported data:

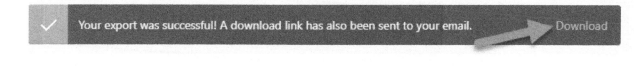

Step 2 – Import the Data into Your WordPress.org Website

You've got your domain setup and WordPress installed (from WordPress.org). Log in to the dashboard of your domain.

From the **Tools** menu in the left sidebar, select **Import**.

At the bottom of the screen, you'll see an option to import from WordPress. This is the option we will use, but first, we need to install a plugin by clicking the **Install Now** link:

Once installed, that **Install Now** link changes to **Run Importer**. Click the Run Importer link. You will be asked to choose a file to import.

The file you downloaded was a zip file. That is a compressed file that you need to unzip first. There are various free tools available that can do this for you, so search Google for a free zip tool if you need one.

Once unzipped, your file will have an XML extension. This is the file we need to import. Click the **Choose file** button and select the unzipped XML file.

Once you have selected the file, click the **Upload File and Import** button.

The next screen will give you the option of supplying an author name for the content.

Import WordPress

Assign Authors

To make it easier for you to edit and save the imported content, you may want to reassign the a may want to import all the entries as `admin` s entries.

If a new user is created by WordPress, a new password will be randomly generated and the new will be necessary.

1. Import author: cabbage2016 (cabbage2016)

   or create new user with login name:

   or assign posts to an existing user: Andy ▾ ←━ ①

Import Attachments

☑ Download and import file attachments ←━ ②

[Submit] ←━ ③

Select the author of the content from the drop-down box, or type in a new user to assign the content to.

Check the box to **Download and import file attachments**.

Now click the **Submit** button.

You should get a message saying:

Import WordPress

All done. Have fun!

Remember to update the passwords and roles of imported users.

If you go to your site, you should find all the posts and pages have been imported into your site.

With all the content across on your hosted domain, you can now choose themes and plugins, and set the site up to look as you want. It should not take you too long to get the site looking the same, or better than before.

Step 3 – Redirect the WordPress.com Site to Your New Domain

Once the content has been moved across, you will have two sites showing identical content. The same articles will be on your WordPress.com site and your hosted domain.

If your WordPress.com site does not have valuable links pointing to it and does not get any real search engine traffic, you can set the site to **Private**.

To do that, log in to your WordPress.com website and click on the **Manage -> Settings** menu. Scroll down to the **Privacy** section and choose **Private**:

Click the **Save Settings** button.

Your site will now only be visible to you, and search engines should start deindexing the content on that site.

If your WordPress.com site gets a lot of traffic from the search engines or has valuable links pointing at it, you should redirect the old site to the new.

The problem is that you do not have access to the .htaccess file on WordPress.com to set up the redirects. The solution is to use a service provided by WordPress.com.

Login to your WordPress.com website and click on the **Manage -> Settings** menu in the left sidebar.

On the setting screen, you will see a section called **Site Address**.

Click on the link to **redirect** this site.

You then have the option of signing up for the redirection service. At the time of writing, this service cost £11 per year.

Once you have the redirect in place, you can forget about your old WordPress.com website. At any time, you can cancel the redirection service, but if you do, make sure you also delete your WordPress.com website or you'll once again have your content duplicated on two websites.

Appendix II. Search Engine Optimization (SEO)

Search Engine Optimization has changed a lot in the last few years. It has always been one of the most important aspects of building a website because it helps you to rank better in Google, and consequently get more traffic, and make more sales from your pages.

Today, things are very different. If you overdo your optimization, Google is likely to penalize you and dump your site out of its search engine.

If you ask Google about the best way to optimize your site, it would probably tell you to avoid Search Engine Optimization altogether, focus on 'visitor experience', and not worry about search engines.

Despite sounding like a lost cause, you should still consider a number of "best practices" as you build your website. I will list the main things to consider here, but if you want a more in-depth discussion about SEO, I'd highly recommend my own book on the subject called **SEO 2019 & Beyond - Search Engine Optimization will never be the same again** (the 2020 version should be out in early 2020). See the resources section later in the book for a link to all my books and courses.

Main Points for Safe SEO

1. Always write content for the visitor, not the search engines.

2. Always create the highest quality content possible and make it unique. More than that, add something to your content that is not found on any other websites covering the same or similar topic. Use your personal voice, experiences, and thoughts.

3. Engage your visitor and allow them to open discussion with you through the built-in comment feature.

4. Never try to write content based on keyword phrases. Always write content on a topic. E.g. don't write an article on "best iPhone case", write an article on "Which iPhone Case offers the best protection for your phone?" See the difference?

5. As a measure of whether your content is good enough, ask yourself if you could imagine your article appearing in a glossy magazine? If you answer no, then it's not good enough to publish on your own website.

6. DO NOT hire people to build backlinks to your site. If you want to build some links, they need to be on high-quality web pages. You can find more specific advice in my SEO book.

7. Add a social sharing plugin to your site so that people can quickly share your content on social channels like Facebook, Twitter, YouTube and Google Plus, etc.

The best advice I can give you for present-day SEO is to **read and digest Google's Webmaster Guidelines**. They are there to help us create sites that will rank well in their Search Engine Results Pages, aka SERPs. You can read those guidelines here:

https://ezseonews.com/wmg

Tasks to Complete

1. Read Google's Webmaster Guidelines repeatedly until you know them off by heart. They really are very important and will benefit you in the long run; providing you adhere to their suggestions of course

Where to Go from Here?

We've covered a lot of ground in this book. You should now be confident in finding your way around the WordPress Dashboard.

You have installed WordPress, installed the essential plugins, and configured everything so that your site is now ready for content.

So, what's the next step?

Create impressive content!

Everything we have done in this book has been to achieve one main goal. Get your site set up & ready to accept your content. You can now concentrate on publishing content while WordPress takes care of the rest.

Here is your plan going forward.

1. Create a post.
2. Publish it.
3. Rinse and repeat steps 1 and 2.

If you want a "static" homepage rather than one showing your recent posts, create a page with the content you want to be displayed there. Then set up the reading settings so that this page is shown permanently on your site's homepage. You can then go back to the 3-step process outlined above

Create a post, publish & repeat.

Good luck!

Andy Williams

Useful Resources

There are a few places that I would recommend you visit for more information.

My Other Webmaster Books

All my books are available as Kindle books and paperbacks. You can view them all here:

https://amazon.com/author/drandrewwilliams

I'll leave you to explore those if you are interested. You'll find books on various aspects of being a webmaster, such as creating high-quality content, SEO, CSS, etc.

My Video Courses

I have a growing number of video courses hosted on Udemy. You can view a complete list of these at my site:

https://ezseonews.com/udemy

There are courses on the same kinds of topics that my books cover, so SEO, Content Creation, WordPress, Website Analytics, etc.

Google Webmaster Guidelines

https://ezseonews.com/wmg - this is the webmaster's bible of what is acceptable and what is not in the eyes of the world's biggest search engine.

Google Analytics

http://www.google.com/analytics/ - the best free analytics program out there. When you have some free time to learn how to use Google Analytics, I recommend you upgrade from Get Clicky.

Wordpress Glossary

This glossary lists some of the technical terms I've used in this book. You may also hear these terms when watching other videos, or tutorials online. Don't let this list scare you. You do not need to know all of these. This list is for reference only. As you go through this book, if you hear a word you don't understand, look here.

Administrator / Admin - The person that is responsible for maintaining the website, adding pages, etc.

Category Silo - A silo is a closely related group of posts that link to each other, but not to less related posts. For example, you might have a category on your site about mountain bikes. All posts in that category are about mountain bikes and link to other articles on mountain bikes. Categories in Wordpress allow you to group posts into these silos, so you might hear the term category silo, simply meaning a group of highly related posts, all in the same category.

cPanel - This is your web host control panel that provides an easy to use interface and automation tools to simplify your job as site admin.

Child Theme - This is a Wordpress theme that inherits its functionality from a parent theme. The parent theme needs to be installed as well as the child theme. Changes made to the child theme won't affect the parent theme, so you can update the parent theme as and when updates are available, without trashing your site.

CSS - The layout and design of a web page and its contents are controlled by CSS. This stands for Cascading Style Sheets. You can change colors, font size, alignment of text or images, etc, all using CSS.

Database - A database is a file that contains information. Wordpress stores your site content and settings in the database.

Dashboard - This is the Wordpress control panel, where you log in to add/edit your website.

Directory (or folder) - You organize files on your computer into folders (also called directories). Web Servers are just computers too and files are organized into directories (or folders) on servers too.

DNS - DNS stands for Domain Name System. It's a system that converts domain names into numeric IP addresses. See also, Registrar and web host.

Domain / Domain Name - This is your website's web address. e.g. mydomain.com

FTP - Stands for File Transfer Protocol. This is a system for connecting to your webspace so you can add, edit, delete files, etc. Using a tool called an FTP client, you can view all files and folders on your server in much the same way you can with a File Explorer on your computer.

.htaccess - This is a file that is processed by your web server before your web page is loaded in a web browser. You can add specific messages to this file, e.g. to prevent certain people accessing your site, or redirecting an old URL to a new URL.

Host - See Web Host

HTTPS - Http defines how content is formatted and transmitted around the web as well as how web servers react to that content. Https is the same as http but uses SSL to ensure content is encrypted.

IP address - This is a unique string of numbers and full stops (periods) that uniquely identify a computer on the internet.

MySQL - This is an open-source database that is commonly used with Wordpress installations as well as other web applications.

Plugins - Plugins are pieces of software that can "plugin" to Wordpress to add new features. e.g. a plugin might allow you to create a contact form or backup your database on a schedule.

Protocol - Essentially a set of rules that define how something works.

Registrar - Also called the domain registrar. This is the company that registers your domain for you. They will renew it if you want to. When someone comes to your website, the registrar will send them to your web host, via the DNS settings at the registrar. Each web host has unique DNS, so the visitor will be sent to your web host, where your Wordpress site is installed.

Responsive Theme - These themes adjust to the size of the web browser. If someone is viewing your site on a mobile phone, the responsive theme makes sure it looks great. The same site in a desktop browser will also look great as the responsive theme adjusts the layout accordingly.

Root folder - This is the top-level folder on your server where a website is installed. On your home computer, the root folder for any application you have installed will be the folder that contains all the files and sub-folders for that application.

RSS Feed - Stands for Rich Site Summary or Really Simple Syndication. It is a file that contains details of the last X posts on your website. Each post will have details of title, date, description, etc.

SEO - Stands for Search Engine Optimization and refers to the methods you use to try to get your site to rank higher in the search engines.

Shortcodes - A Wordpress specific code that you can use to insert something into a website. E.g. a contact form plugin may give you a shortcode like [cf-form-1]. when the page is rendered in the browser, the shortcode is replaced by the contact form.

SSL - Stands for Secure Sockets Layer. It's a security measure to ensure a connection between two computers is encrypted.

Themes - These are the "skins" of your site. They control the fonts, colors & layout of your site. You can change the look and feel of your site by changing the theme. It takes seconds to do.

URL - the web address you type into your web browser.

Web Host - This is the company that rents you disk space on their computers (servers). You can use that disk space to install your website. When someone visits your website, it's delivered from that web host. The web host has a unique DNS that you give to your registrar.

Webmaster - Same as administrator.

wp-config.php - This file contains the basic setup information for your Wordpress site. Things like database name and other database settings.

Widgets - These are plug and play pieces of software that can add features to various areas of your website. e..g there is a widget that displays a calendar and this could be placed in the sidebar.

Please Leave a Review/Thought on Amazon

If you enjoyed this book, or even if you didn't, I'd love to hear your comments about it. You can leave your thoughts on the Amazon website.

Index